Johnny Smith

GLOSSARY OF CONTENTS

GLOSSARY OF CONTENTS

PART ONE

— Foreword —

The guitar is a remarkable instrument in many ways. Having variable timbre, it can blend harmoniously with any instrument in the musical family. It's versatility is unique because it can be used as a warm or exciting solo voice and/or a complete accompaniment instrument. It is, therefor, understandable that the guitar is being written for and used more and more as time goes on. Composers and arrangers are more and more convinced that including the guitar in their works can do nothing but enhance and enrichen the value and acceptance of their products.

The guitarist who meets the demands of the instrument has to be a unique musician to measure up to the unique instrument he plays. He has to be a versatile musician to cover the wide range of uses expected of the guitar. As the standards for the guitar continue to rise, the proficiency of the guitarists will have to do likewise. This can only be possible by the guitar player having thorough knowledge and understanding of the guitar and of music itself.

INTRODUCTION TO BASIC FORM MAJOR MINOR CHORDS AND SCALES

Thorough knowledge of the guitar fingerboard is very difficult to acquire because of the different fingering and position possibilities for playing not only melodic passages but groups of notes (chords).

For example, there are at least ten different ways to finger and places to play this one octave C scale:

(Actual Pitch)

There are at least four places to play this one C major triad:

(Actual Pitch)

The basic form two-octave scale studies are directly related to, what I refer to as, basic form major and minor chords. These chords are root position chords, that is, the chords will be called from the bottom note.

The scales are diatonic major and harmonic minor. The reason for choosing the harmonic minor is that this minor scale is the most commonly used of the minor scales. The basic form chords learned throughout the entire cycle of keys, serves as a comprehensive method for establishing basic knowledge of the fingerboard from which the other types of chords can be learned and remembered. Building between the basic forms (inversions) can then be accomplished with a minimum of effort and confusion.

The basic form two octave scales studies are not only helpful melodically but, learned throughout the entire cycle, contribute to the knowledge of the fingerboard and are extremely valuable as a daily practice sequence for building an exacting technique.

The notation in this, and subsequent, books will be in *actual pitch* using bass and treble clefs. Many composers prefer to write for the guitar in this way as shown in the excerpts below:

SERENADE OP. 24 (5th Movement)

ARNOLD SCHOENBERG (1923)

CONCERTO IN ONE MOVEMENT
FOR ELECTRIC GUITAR AND ORCHESTRA

MAX DI JULIO (1968)

One of the contributing factors in the misnaming, misuse and misunderstanding of chords has been the misconception that the guitar is strictly a treble clef instrument.

As an example of confusion brought about by this misconception, take the group of four notes shown below. This group of notes can be six different chords, and each chord would have a different use. The only way this confusion can be eliminated is to understand *all* chords by their bass notes, which are generally located in the bass clef.

Example

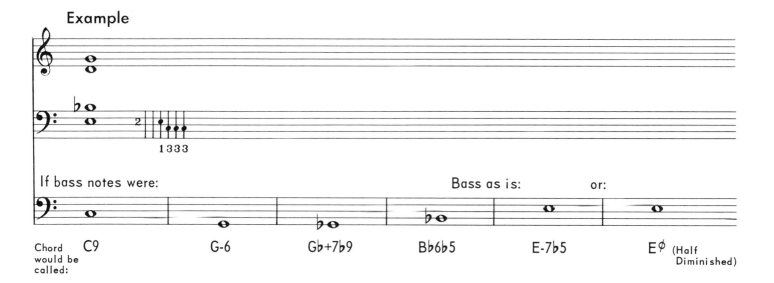

| Chord would be called: | C9 | G-6 | Gb+7b9 | Bb6b5 | E-7b5 | Eø (Half Diminished) |

The difference between the minor seventh flat five and the half diminished is in the way they resolve. For example: The E-7b5 would resolve to the IV7 (A7). If the resolution were to E° or E7 or to any other chord other than A7, the chord would be called a half diminished. The important thing is the fact that each one of these chords would resolve in a different way.

The C9 would most likely resolve to F. The G-6 would not resolve. (6th or minor 6th chords are not considered resolving chords.) The Gb +7b9 would most likely resolve to B9 or B$^6_9$. The Bb 6 b5 would usually resolve to a seventh chord one-half step lower: (Bb 6 b5 ⟶ A7). The E-7 b5 and Eø as explained above. The most frequently used bass progressions are fourth steps (IV) and half steps (½). This being true, we would choose two of the chords shown above to lead into A7.

$$E - 7 \flat 5 \longrightarrow A7 \text{ (Fourth Step)}$$
$$B \flat 6 \flat 5 \longrightarrow A7 \text{ (Half Step)}$$

The choice would depend primarily on the melody note (avoiding doubling bass with melody whenever possible) or on the composer or arranger's personal choice. By understanding the simple bass note resolutions, the potential confusion of the above example is immediately eliminated.

There are numerous advantages in having knowledge of the bass as well as the treble clefs. For one thing, it opens up a new realm of music literature and helps to break the bonds that tie the serious guitarist to the music written or transcribed only for the guitar.

The standard range of the guitar (transposed)

E F F# G G# A A# B C C# D D# E F F# G G# A A# B C C# D D#

E F F# G G# A A# B C C# D D# E F F# G G# A A# B C

The standard range of the guitar (actual pitch)

E F Gb G Ab A Bb B C Db D Eb E F Gb G Ab A Bb B C

Db D Eb E F Gb G Ab A Bb B C Db D Eb E F Gb G Ab A Bb B C

Because of the predominance of fourth step progressions used in tonal music, these studies are arranged in a cycle of fourths.

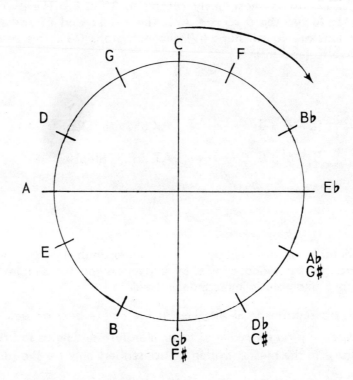

The major chords are the first, third and fifth notes of a diatonic scale.

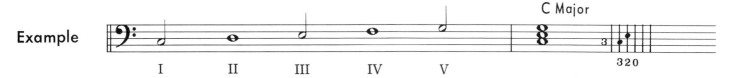

Example

I   II   III   IV   V   C Major

The minor chords are the first, Flat third and fifth notes of a diatonic scale.

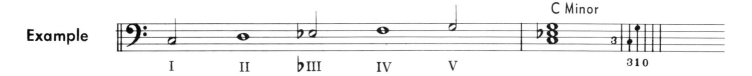

Example

I   II   ♭III   IV   V   C Minor

(note that the C — chord was made from a C scale, not from the E flat scale)

All chords other than Augmented and Diminished are made in a similar way and it is very helpful to know the numerical formulas for the various chords. This knowledge makes it possible to figure out chords that may not have been known by the player previously.

This book has been written in the hopes that the arrangement of chords, scales and inversions will be of help to the serious guitar student in acquiring this knowledge.

Basic Form Major and Minor Chords
(ROOT POSITION)

C Major

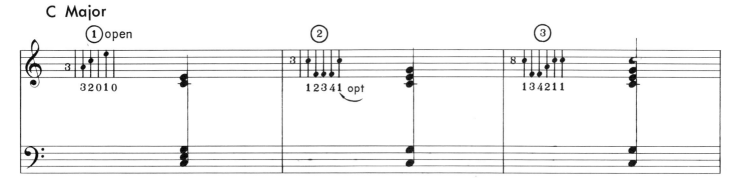

(open) after a chord form or scale from number means that the chord form or scale has open string or strings and generally applies to the First Position.

A Minor

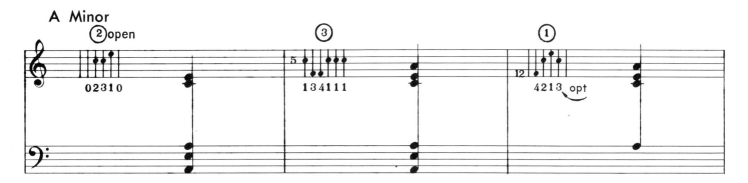

F Major

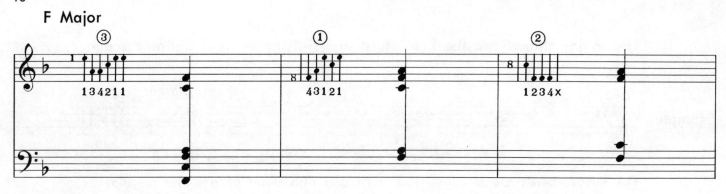

D Minor

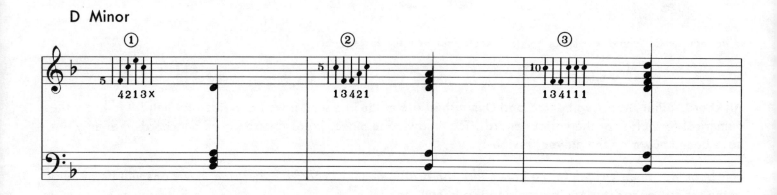

B♭ Major

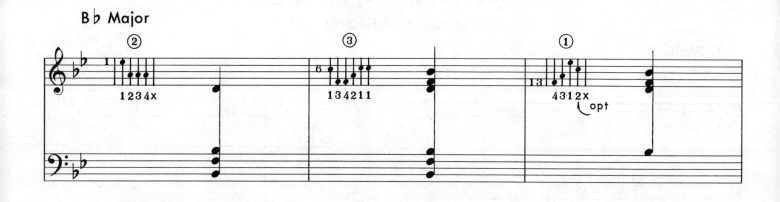

G Minor

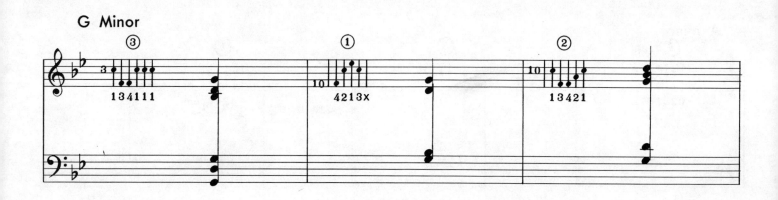

E♭ Major

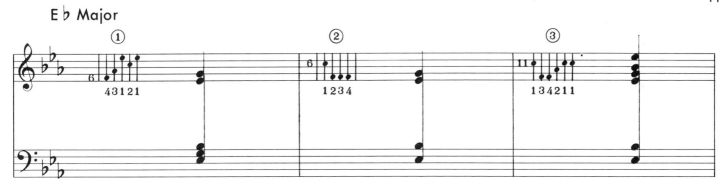

C Minor

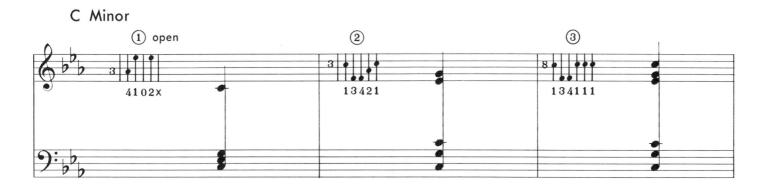

A♭ Major

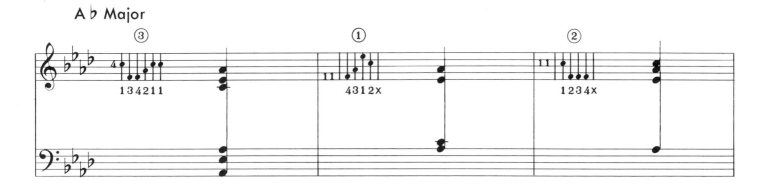

F Minor

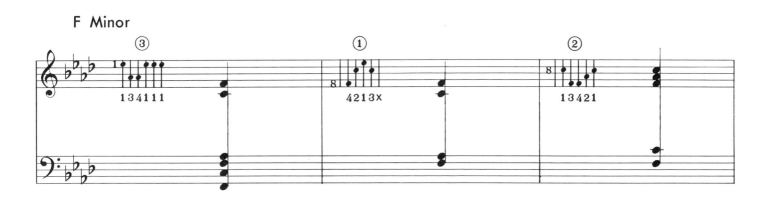

12

Db Major

Bb Minor

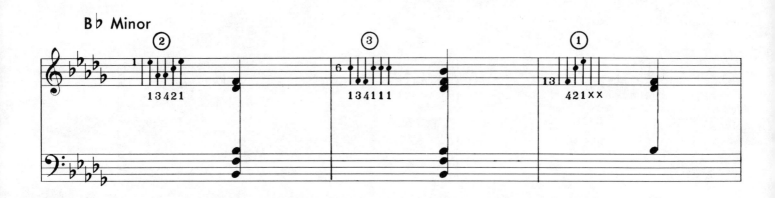

Gb (F#)

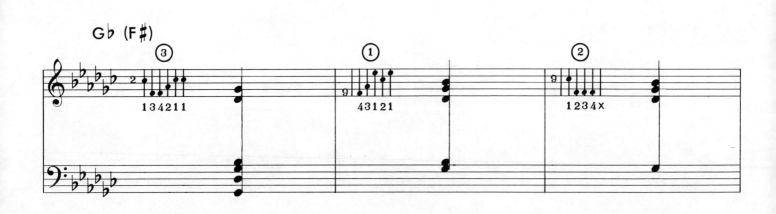

Eb Minor (D#-)

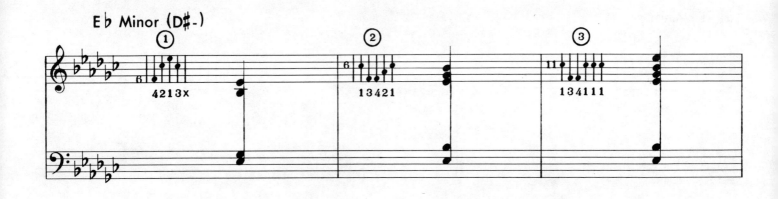

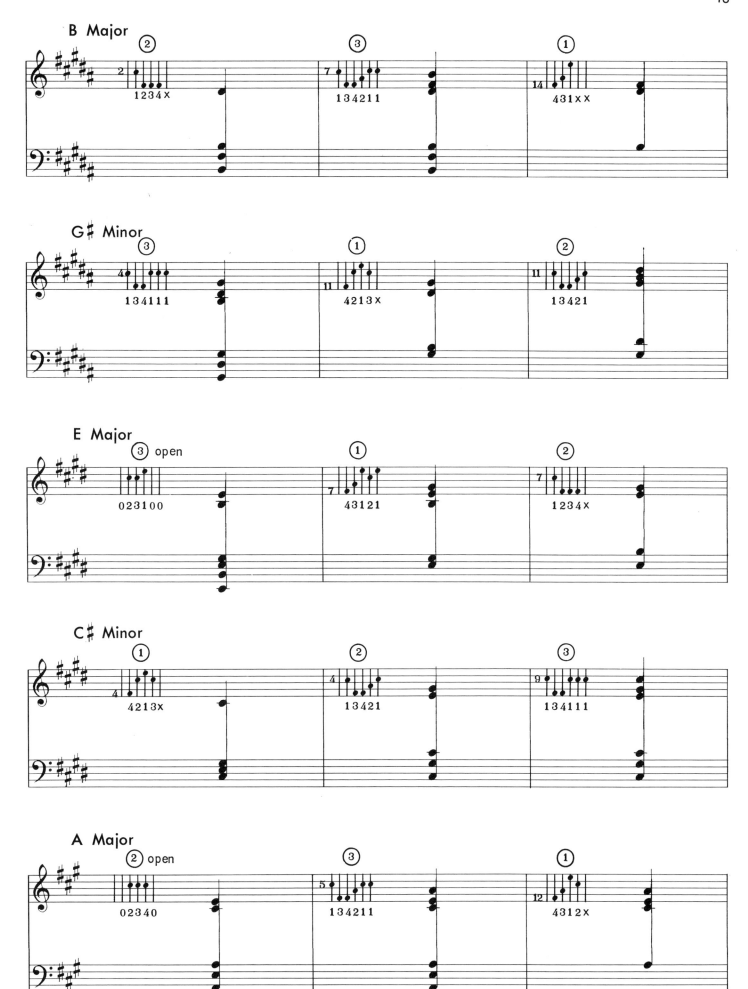

Basic Form Major And Minor Chord Practice Sequence ---

(The chord forms and positions should be memorized)

	Major					Relative Minor			
C major	(1)	open	(2)	(3)	A minor	(2)	open	(3)	(1)
F major	(3)		(1)	(2)	D minor	(1)		(2)	(3)
Bb major	(2)		(3)	(1)	G minor	(3)		(1)	(2)
Eb major	(1)		(2)	(3)	C minor	(1)	open	(2)	(3)
Ab major	(3)		(1)	(2)	F minor	(3)		(1)	(2)
Db major	(1)		(2)	(3)	Bb minor	(2)		(3)	(1)
Gb major	(3)		(1)	(2)	Eb minor	(1)		(2)	(3)
B major	(2)		(3)	(1)	G# minor	(3)		(1)	(2)
E major	(3)	open	(1)	(2)	C# minor	(1)		(2)	(3)
A major	(2)	open	(3)	(1)	F# minor	(3)		(1)	(2)
D major	(1)		(2)	(3)	B minor	(2)		(3)	(1)
G major	(3)		(1)	(2)	E minor	(3)	open	(1)	(2)

Basic Form Two Octave Major and Harmonic Minor Scales

The basic form major scales are related directly to the basic form major chords and, like the chords, are built around forms ①, ②, and ③. Without open strings, these forms can be moved chromatically. The scale forms using open strings are:

①   C Major
③   E major
③   F major
②   A major
②   B flat major

Familiarization of the three closed forms prior to working through the cycle of keys, will simplify the learning of the scales.

Basic form ① can be played chromatically up from D flat major. This form involves a whole step interval shift at the top and is written numerically as follows: (D flat as example)

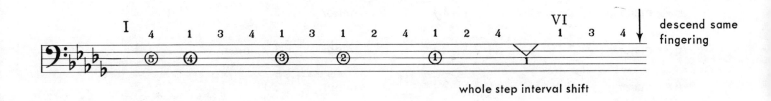

Basic form ②, used chromatically up from B natural involves a half step interval shift midway through the exercise and a whole tone interval shift at the top. It is written as follows: (D flat as example)

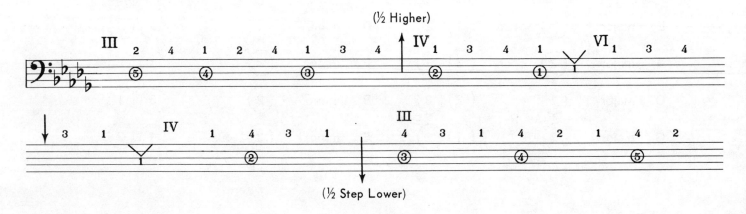

Basic form ③, used chromatically up from G flat, involves no position shift and is, by far, the easiest of the three. Basic form ③: (G flat as example)

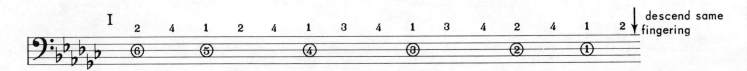

Basic form harmonic minor scales are closely related to the basic form minor chords and forms ① and
② require a minor third interval fingering at the top of the scale.

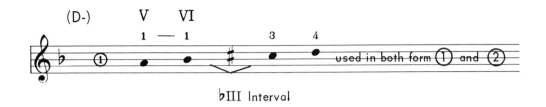

Example (D- form ①)

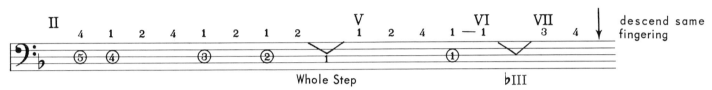

Example (D- form ②)

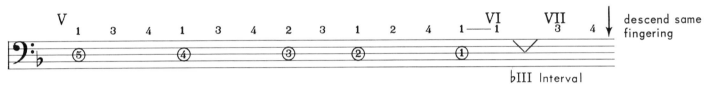

Basic form ③ harmonic minor scale requires a half step position shift (lower) ascending and a half step (higher) descending.

Example (G- Form ③)

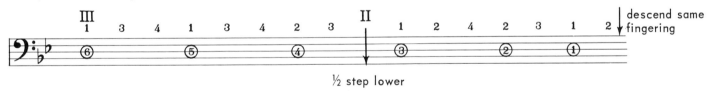

Harmonic minor scale forms using open strings are:
① C minor
③ E minor
③ F minor
② A minor

Circled numbers places in the staff [⑥] indicates the string to be played.
Circled numbers, usually outside the staff [form ③] indicates the chord or scale form.
Roman numerals [IX] indicates the position or fret number that the index finger is placed.

Basic Form Two Octave Major and Harmonic Minor Scales

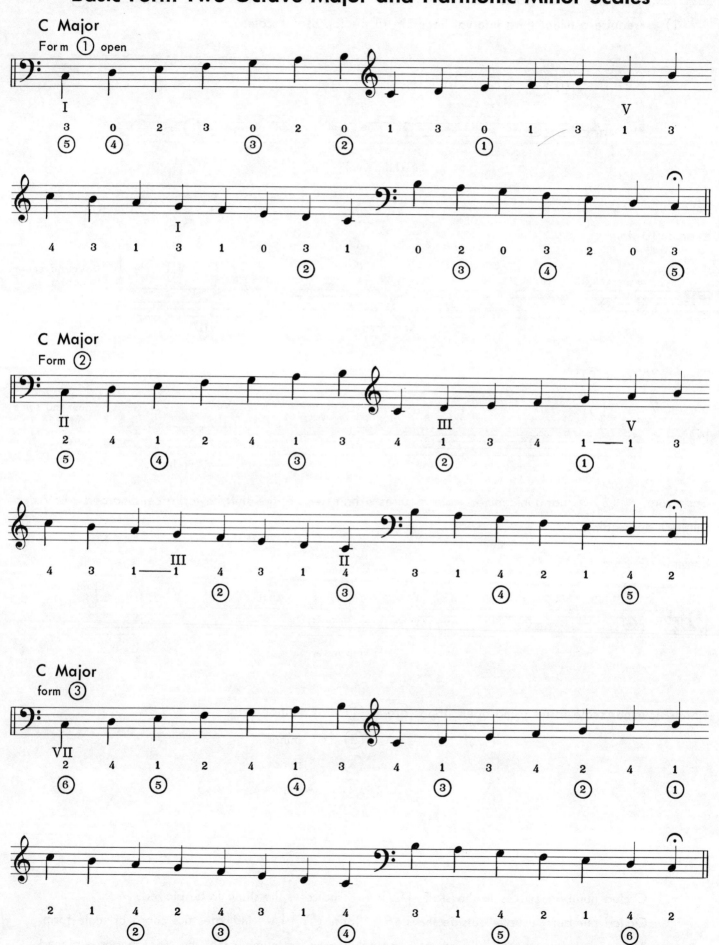

A Minor
Form ② open

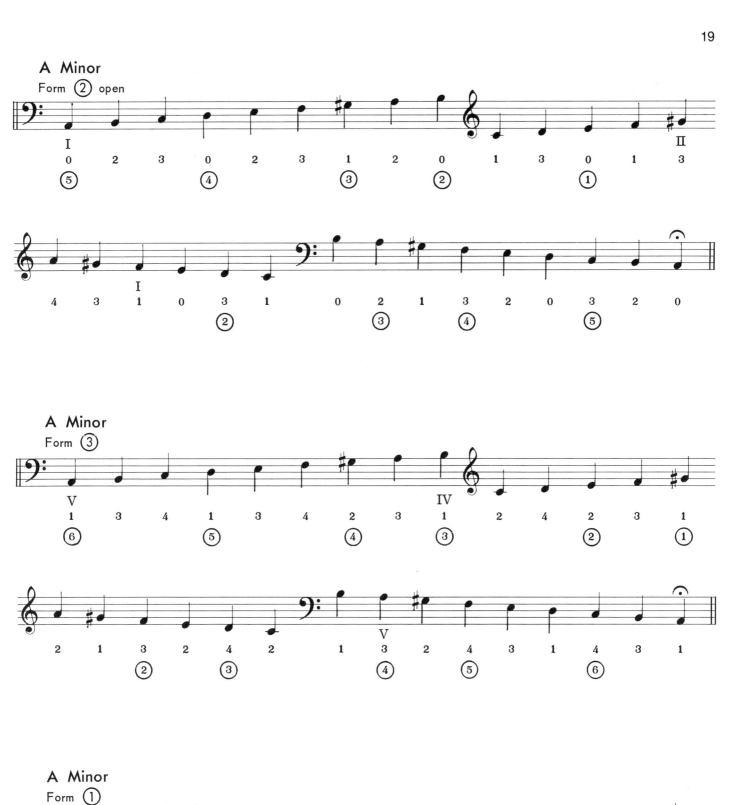

A Minor
Form ①

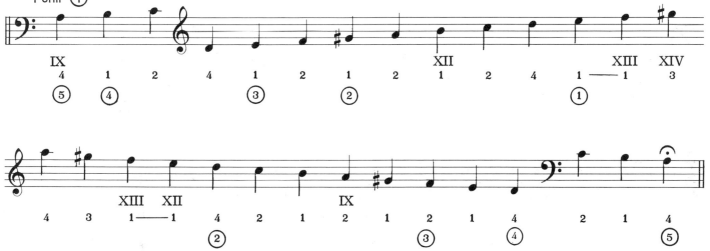

F Major

Form ③ open

F Major

Form ①

F Major

Form ②

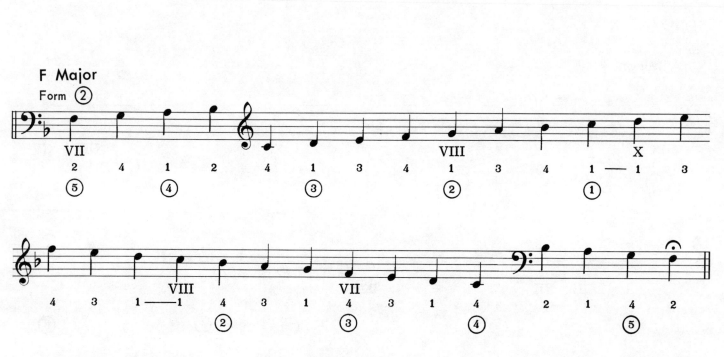

21

D Minor
Form ①

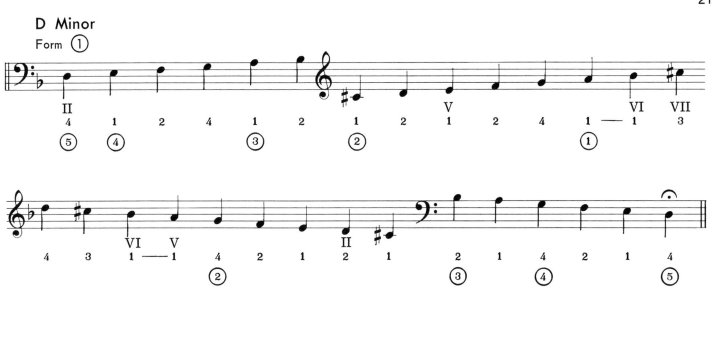

D Minor
Form ②

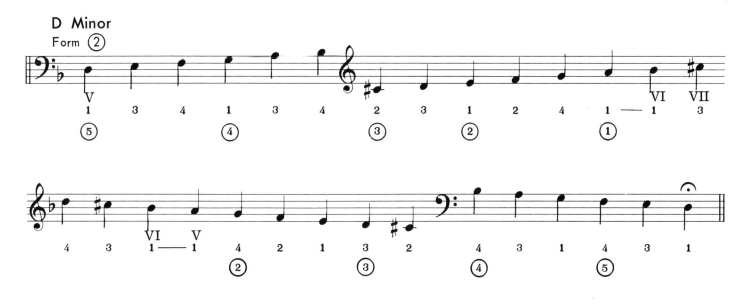

D Minor
Form ③

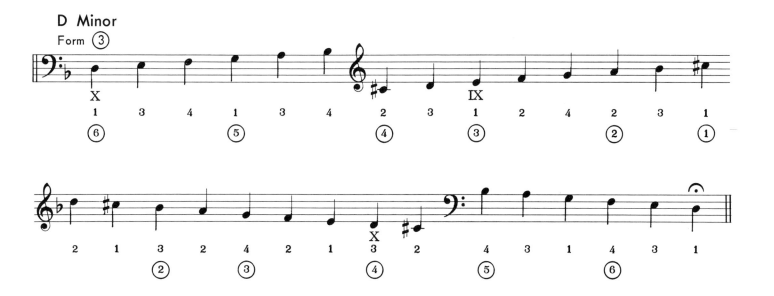

22

Bb Major
Form ② open

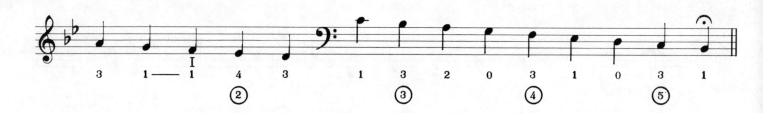

Bb Major
Form ③

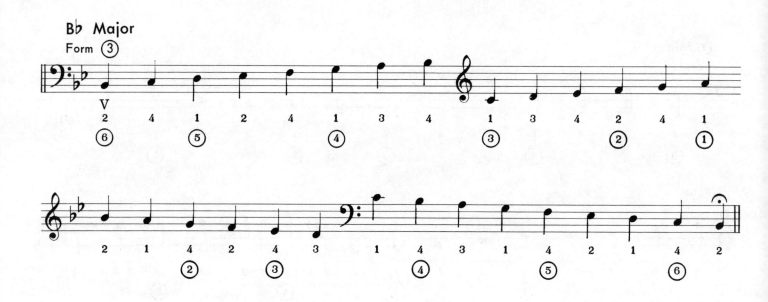

Bb Major
Form ①

Note fingering change (123) instead of (134) at the top of the scale to make the fingering easier in the extreme high positions.

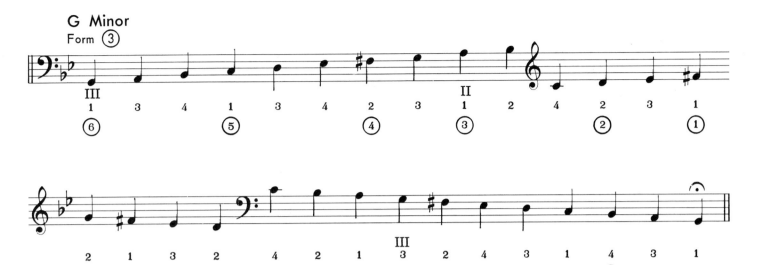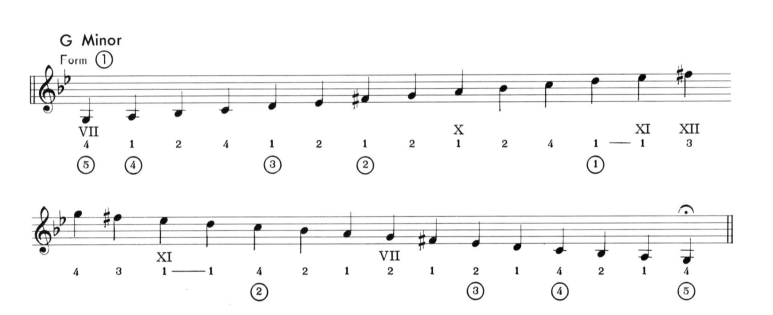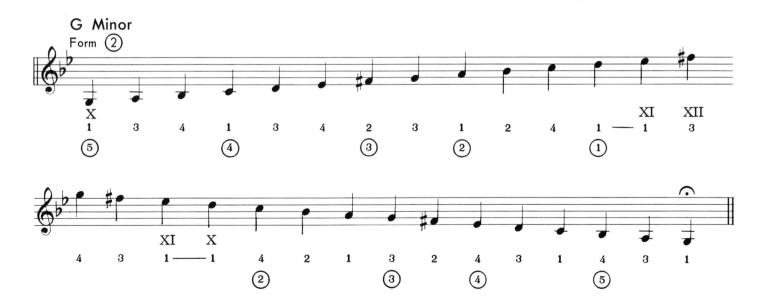

Eb Major
Form ①

Eb Major
Form ②

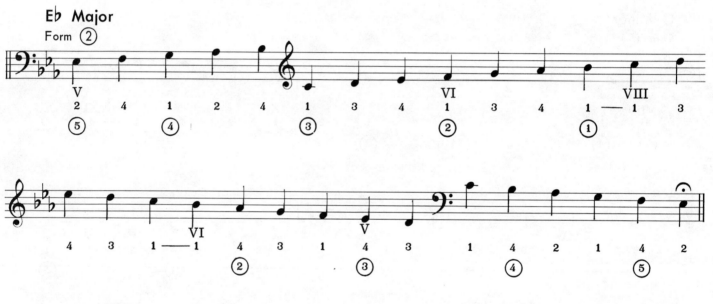

Eb Major
Form ③

C Minor
Form ① open

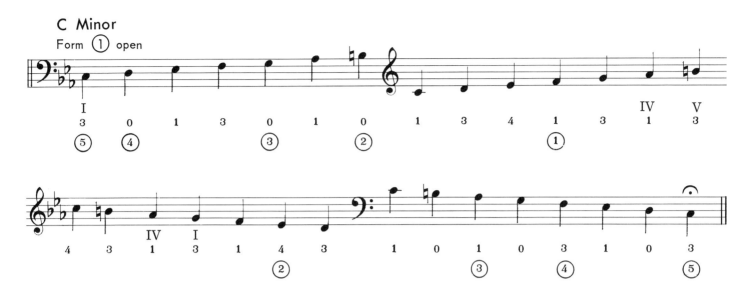

C Minor
Form ②

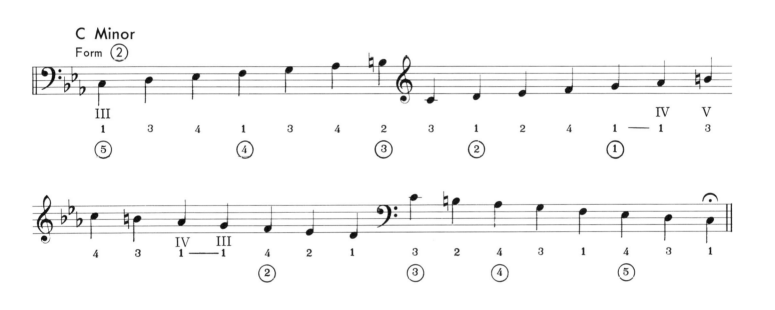

C Minor
Form ③

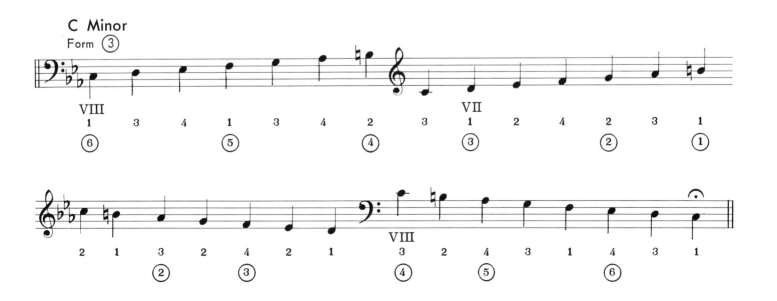

26

Ab Major

Form ③

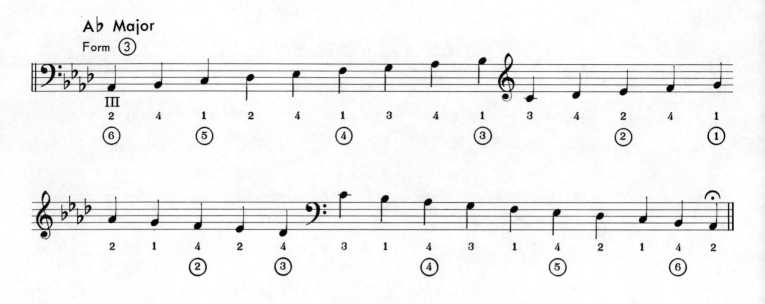

Form ①

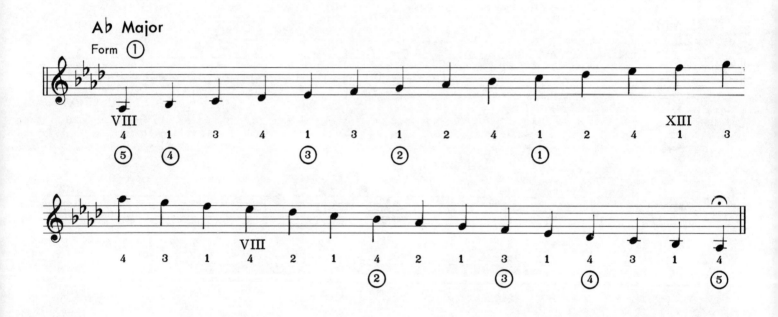

Form ②

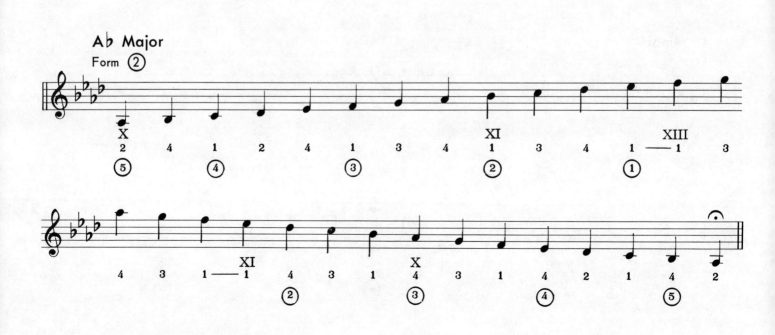

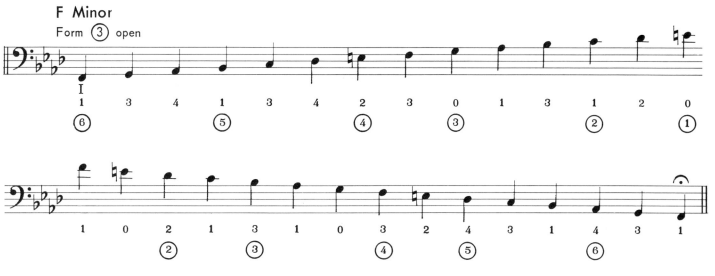

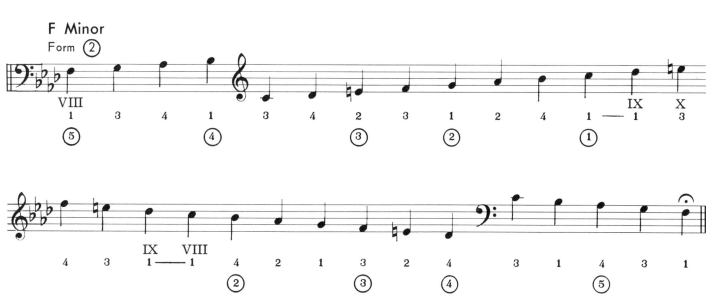

28

Db Major

Form ①

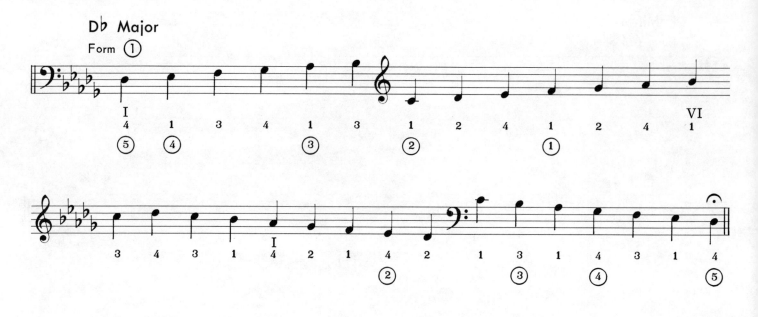

Db Major

Form ②

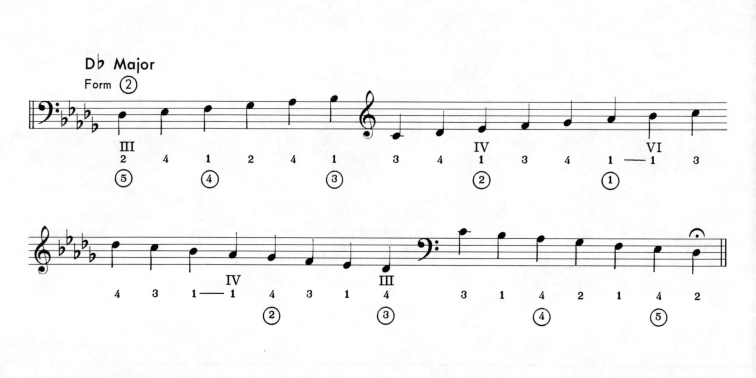

Db Major

Form ③

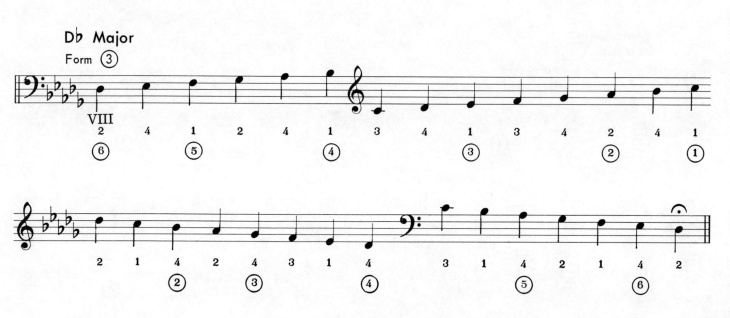

Bb Minor

Form ②

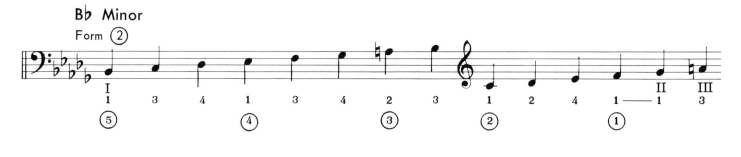

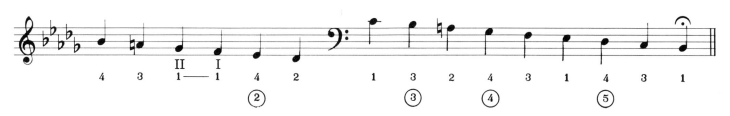

Bb Minor

Form ③

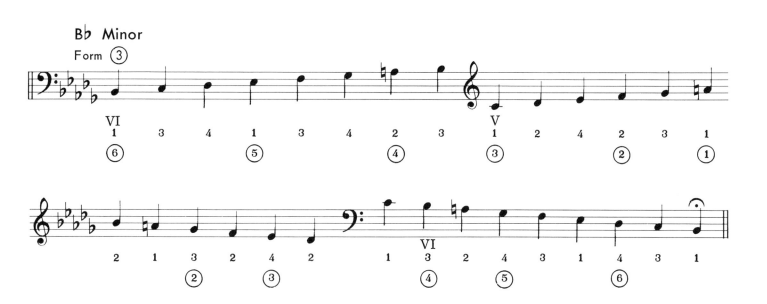

Bb Minor

Form ①

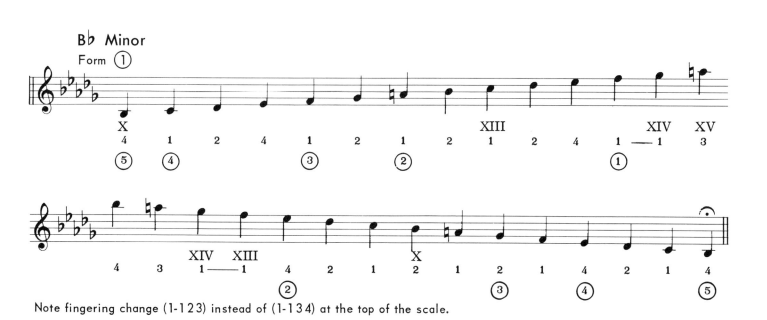

Note fingering change (1-1 2 3) instead of (1-1 3 4) at the top of the scale.

30

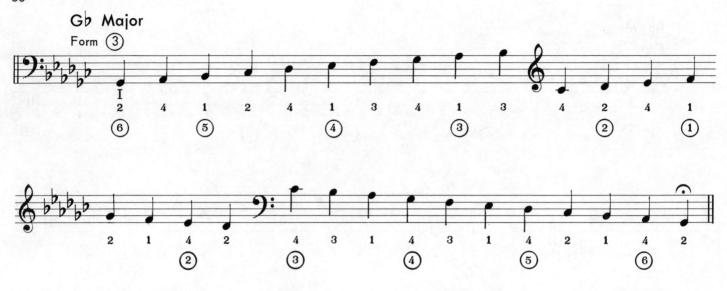

Gb Major

Form ③

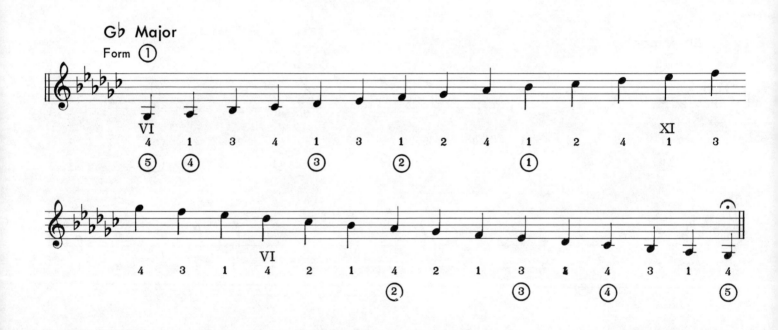

Gb Major

Form ①

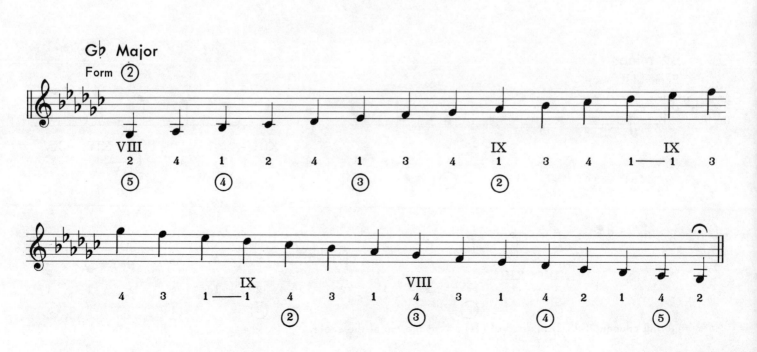

Gb Major

Form ②

Eb Minor
Form ①

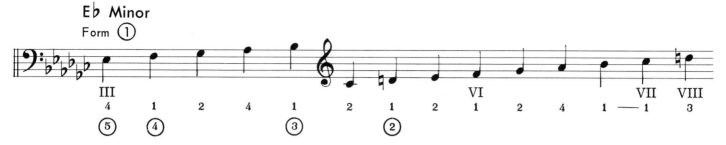

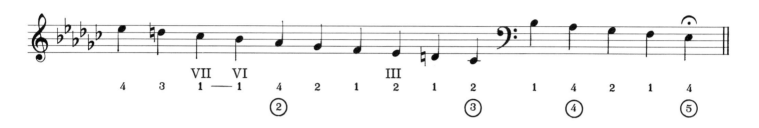

Eb Minor
Form ②

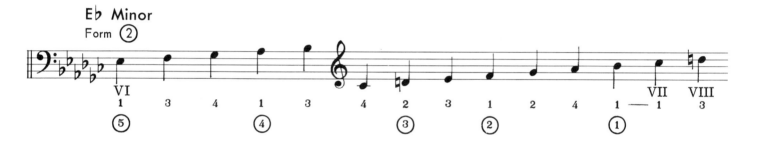

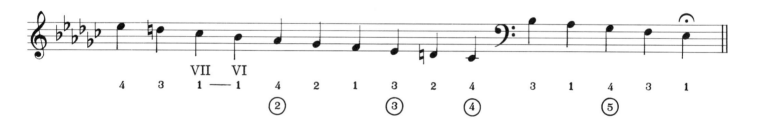

Eb Minor
Form ③

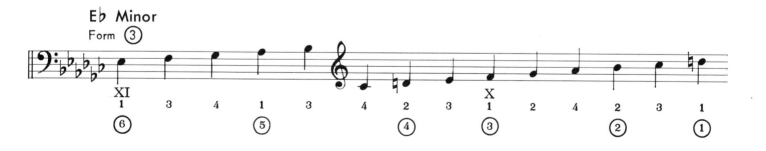

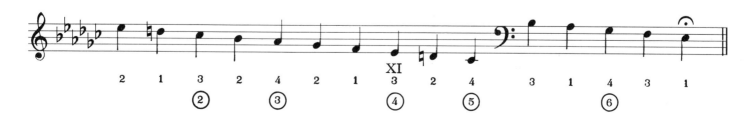

32

B Major

Form ②

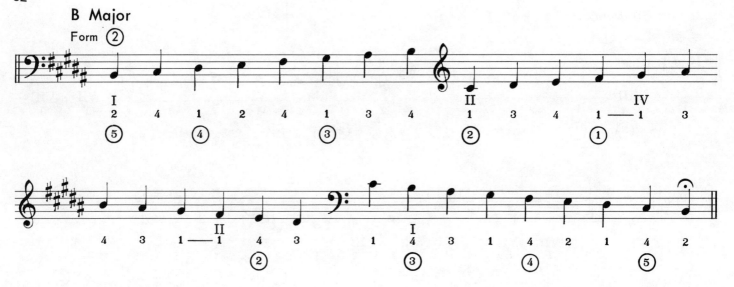

B Major

Form ③

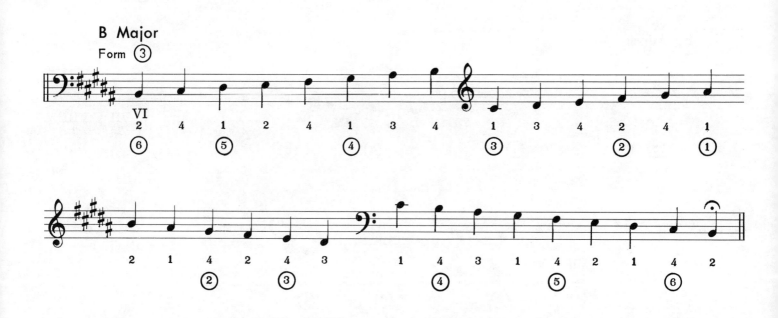

B Major

Form ①

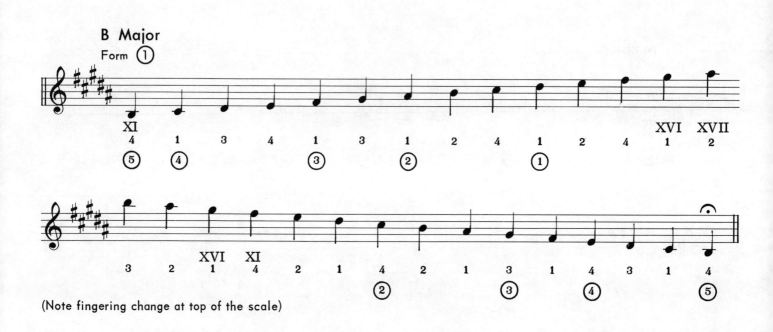

(Note fingering change at top of the scale)

G# Minor

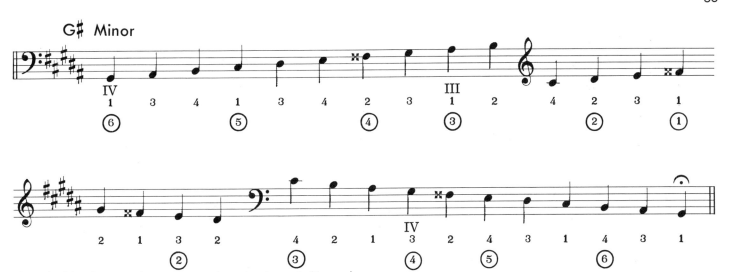

(✗ = double sharp or the note is to be raised two halfsteps)

G# Minor
Form ①

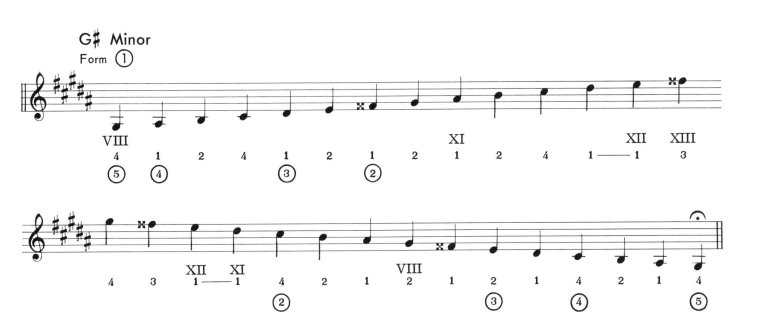

G# Minor
Form ②

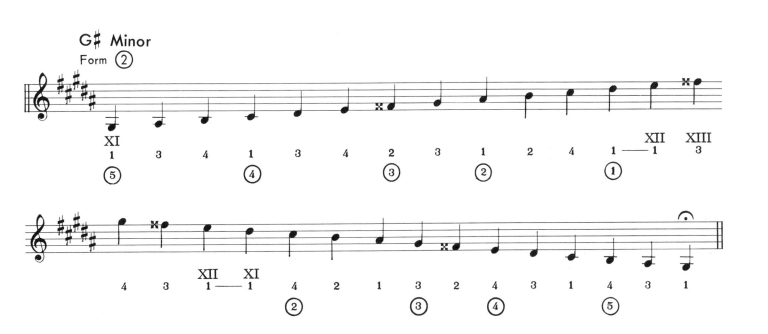

34

E Major

Form ③ open

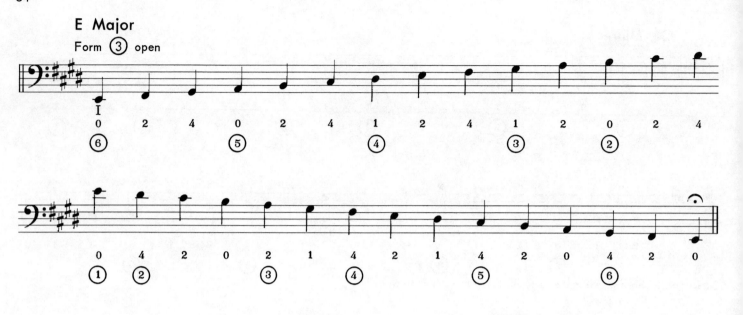

E Major

Form ①

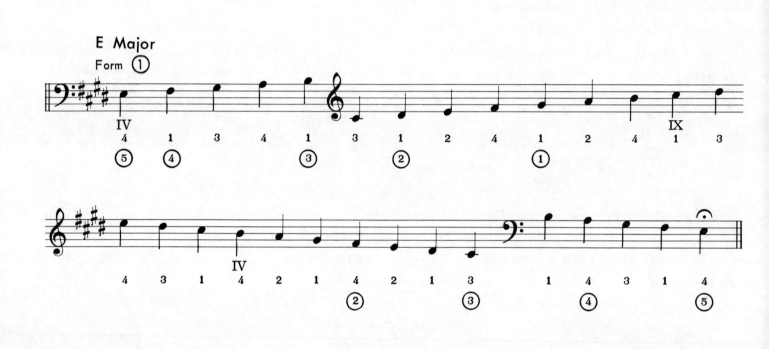

E Major

Form ②

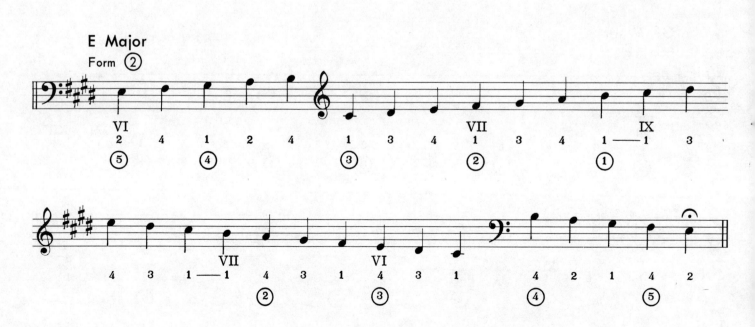

C# Minor
Form ①
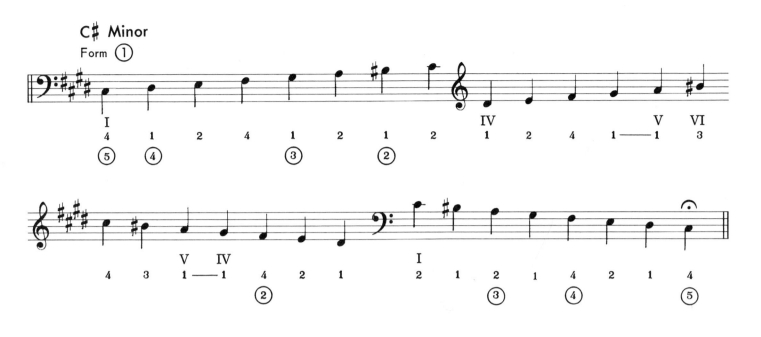

C# Minor
Form ②
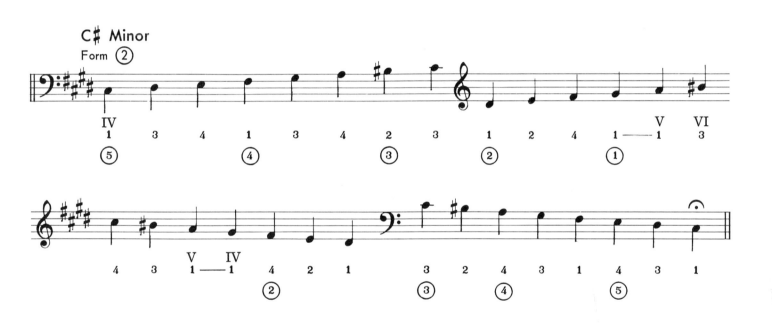

C# Minor
Form ③
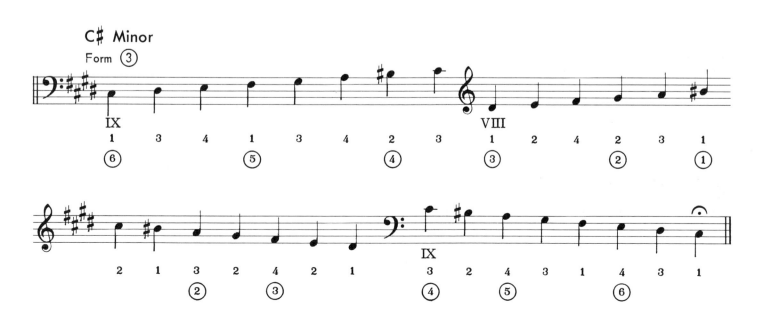

A Major
Form ② open

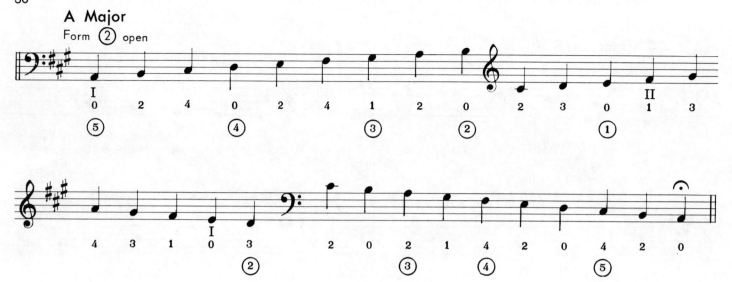

A Major
Form ③

A Major
Form ①

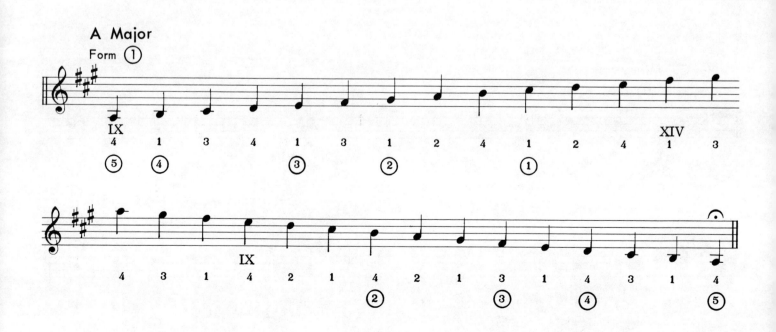

F# Minor
Form ③

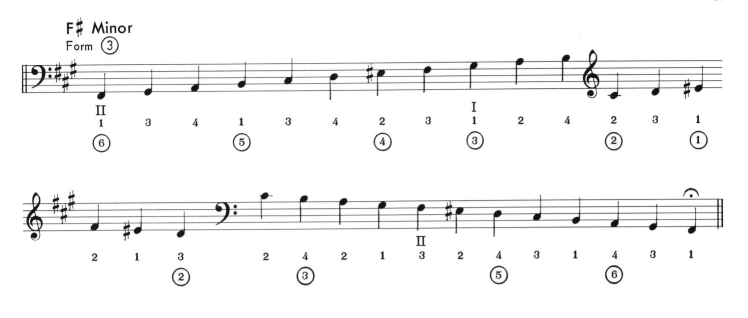

F# Minor
Form ①

F# Minor
Form ②

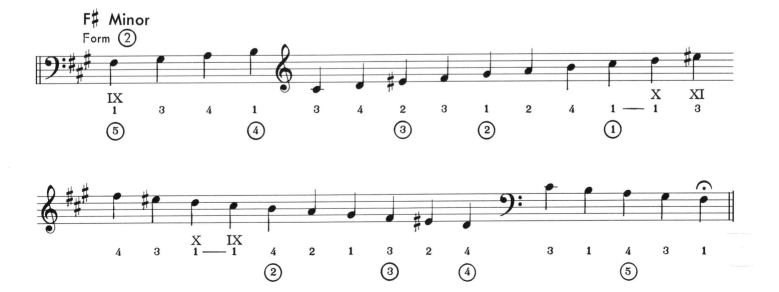

38

D Major
Form ①

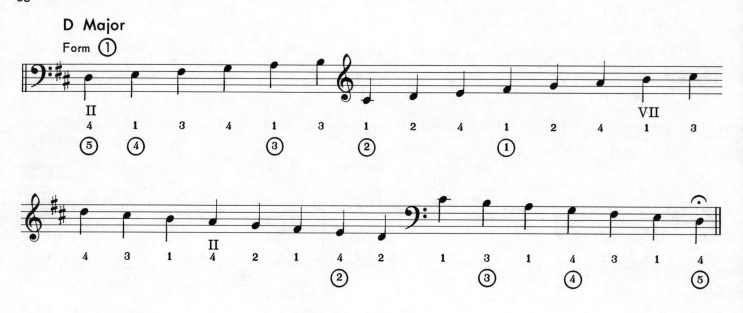

D Major
Form ②

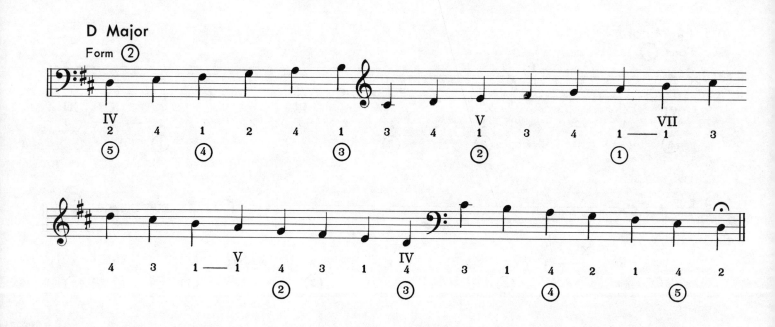

D Major
Form ③

B Minor
Form ②

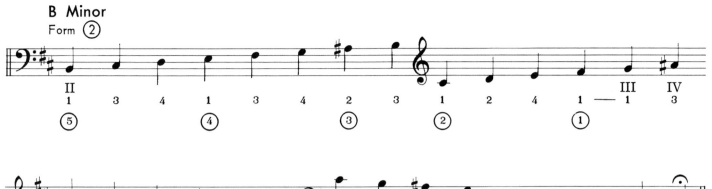

B Minor
Form ③

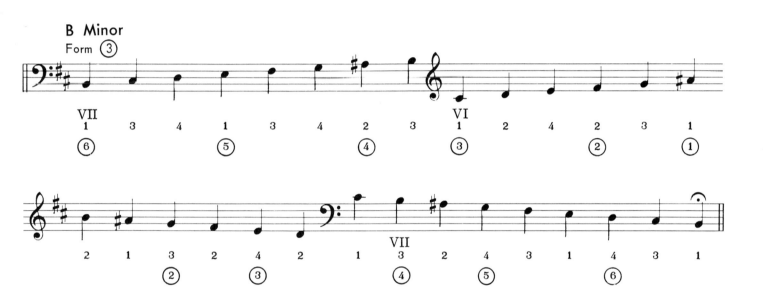

B Minor
Form ①

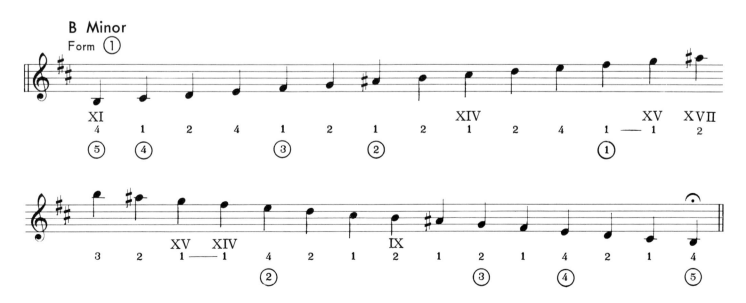

(Note fingering change at top of scale)

40

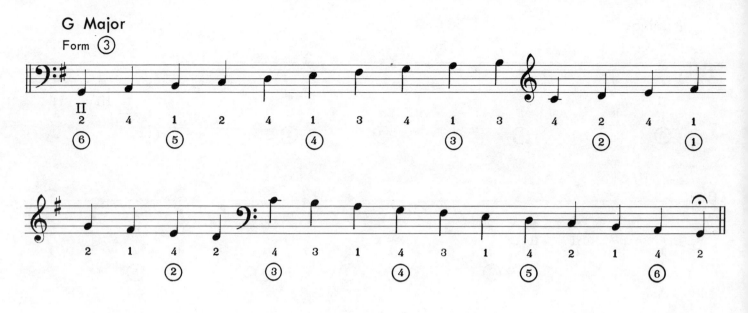

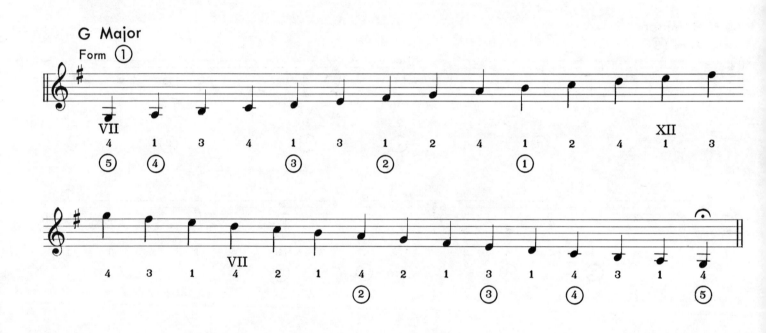

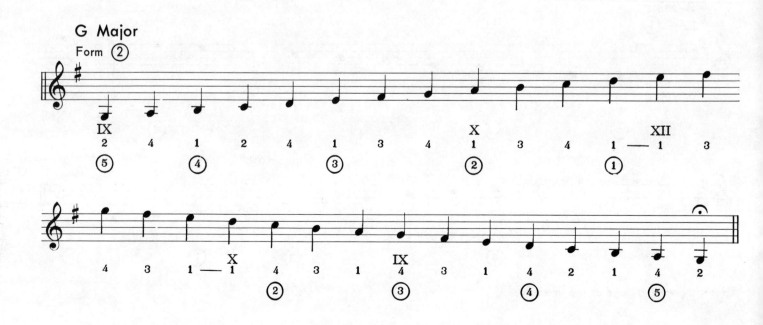

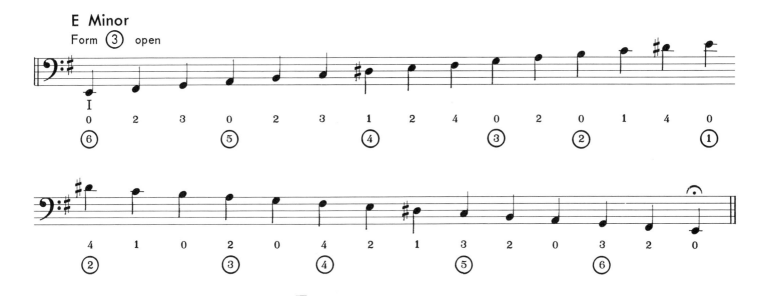

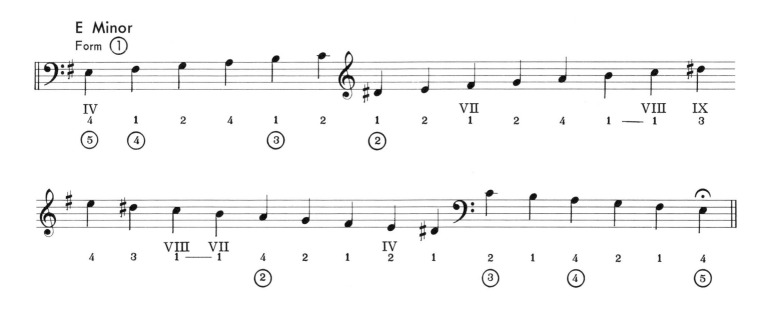

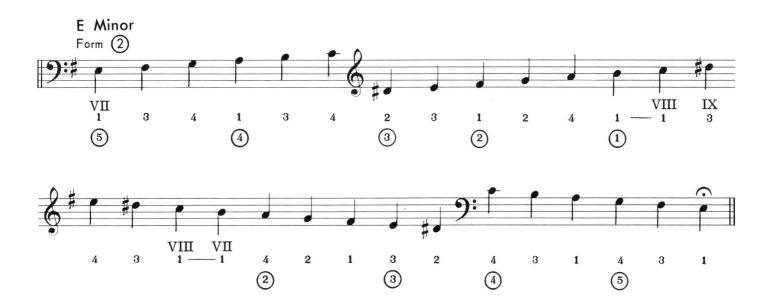

Major and Minor Scales
Practice Sequence
(Entire sequence should be memorized)

Major					Relative Minor				
C	(1)	open	(2)	(3)	A—	(2)	open	(3)	(1)
F	(3)	open	(1)	(2)	D—	(1)		(2)	(3)
Bb	(2)	open	(3)	(1)	G—	(3)		(1)	(2)
Eb	(1)		(2)	(3)	C—	(1)	open	(2)	(3)
Ab	(3)		(1)	(2)	F—	(3)	open	(1)	(2)
Db	(1)		(2)	(3)	Bb—	(2)		(3)	(1)
Gb	(3)		(1)	(2)	Eb—	(1)		(2)	(3)
B	(2)		(3)	(1)	G#—	(3)		(1)	(2)
E	(3)	open	(1)	(2)	C#—	(1)		(2)	(3)
A	(2)	open	(3)	(1)	F#—	(3)		(1)	(2)
D	(1)		(2)	(3)	B—	(2)		(3)	(1)
G	(3)		(1)	(2)	E—	(3)	open	(1)	(2)

MAJOR AND MINOR TRIAD INVERSIONS

Knowledge of the major and minor triads and their inversions is necessary when harmonizing melodies and counter melodies. They are invaluable as component parts of many of the more intricate harmonizations.

Take as an example, a G13 ♭ 9:

The E major triad in the upper structure of this chord can serve as a simple component to work with in constructing a melodic line to fit the sound of this chord. By inverting this triad, a harmonized arpeggio is a very simple procedure (provided you are familiar with the inversions).

An example of a minor triad (A♭-) can be found in the upper voices of a G +7 ♭9 chord.

As an example:

It now becomes apparent that the major and minor triads and their inversions have uses far beyond the major and minor chords themselves. As you study these inversions you will notice that they follow a rotation pattern. This will help in the memorization of these triads on the different strings throughout the entire cycle.

Major and Minor Triad Inversions

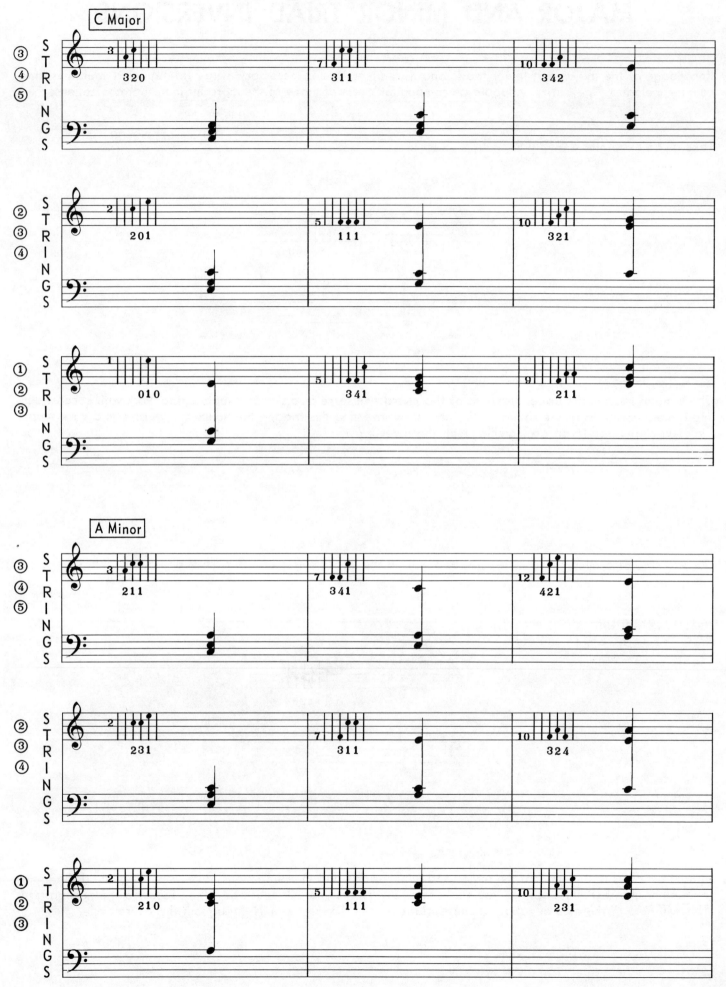

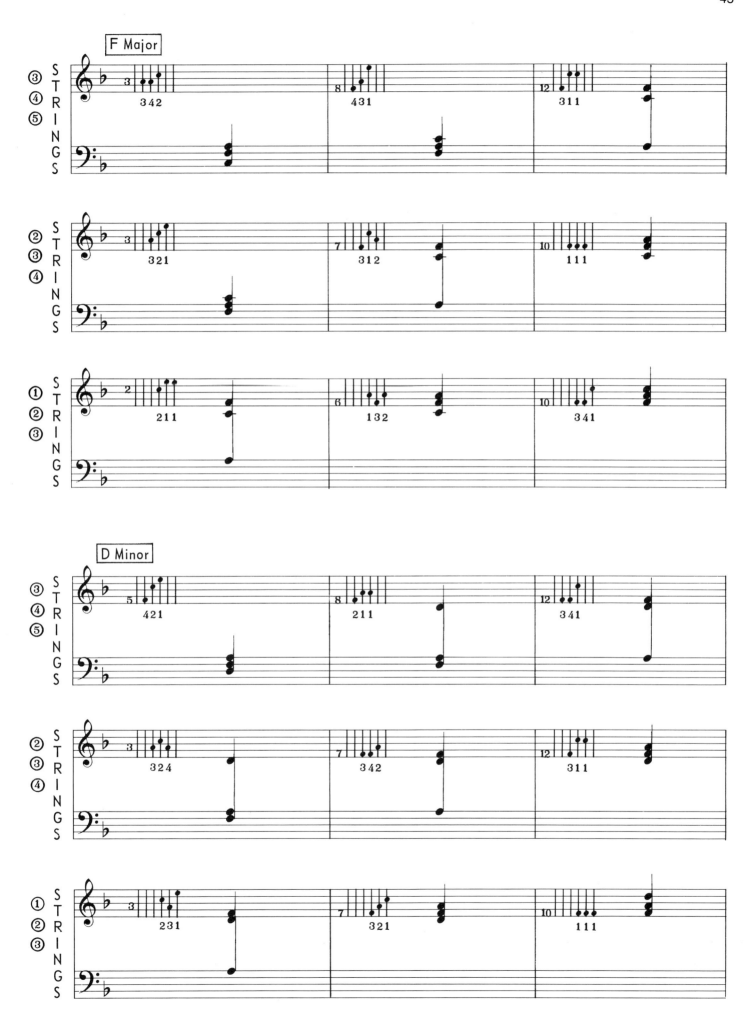

47

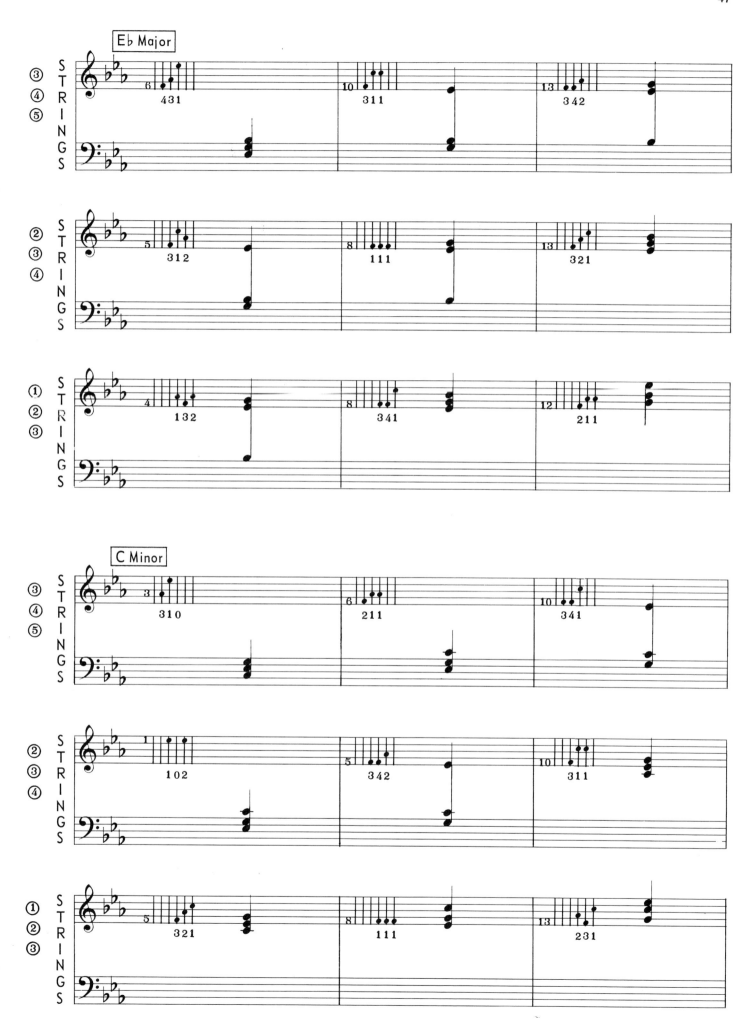

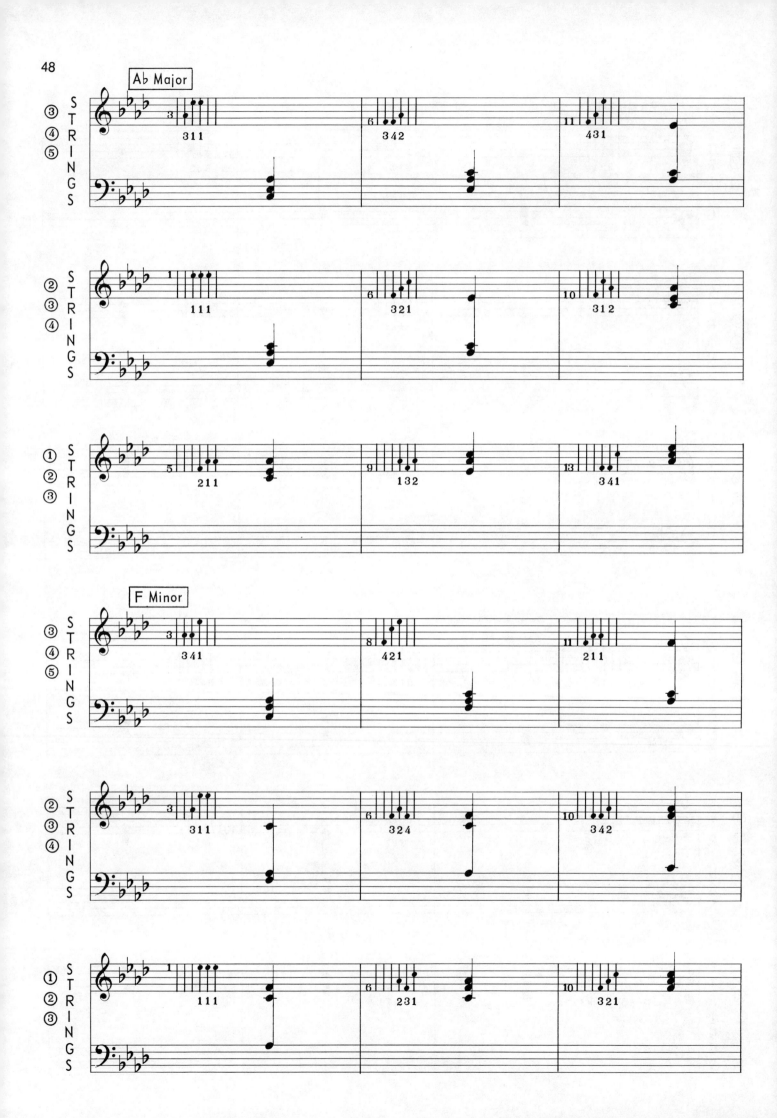

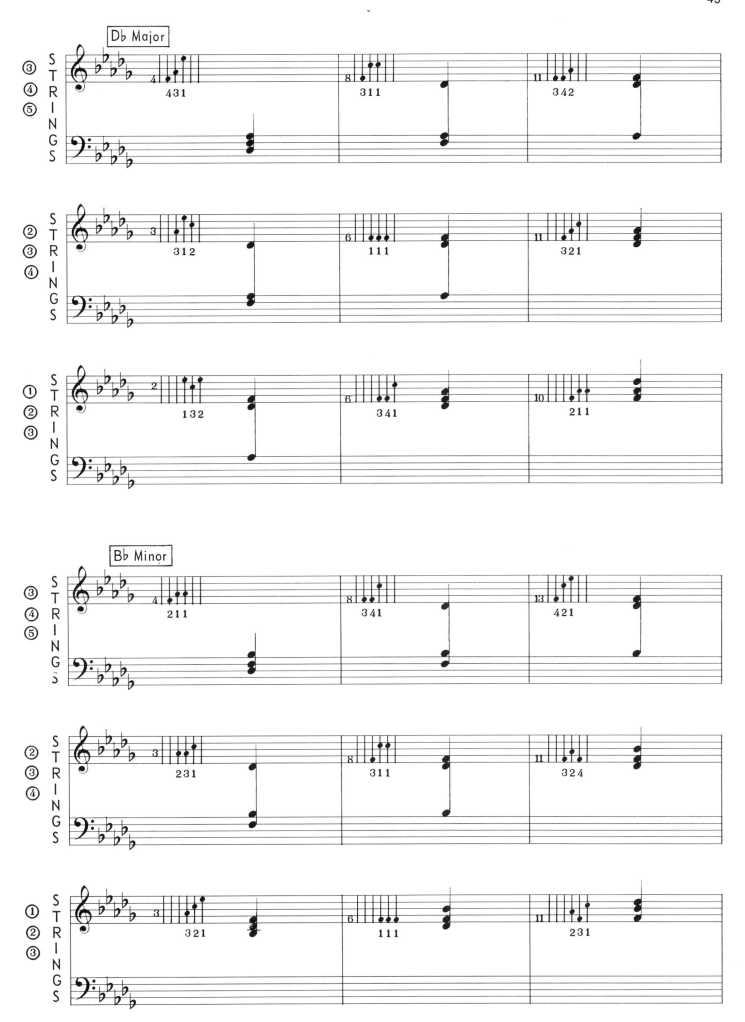

50

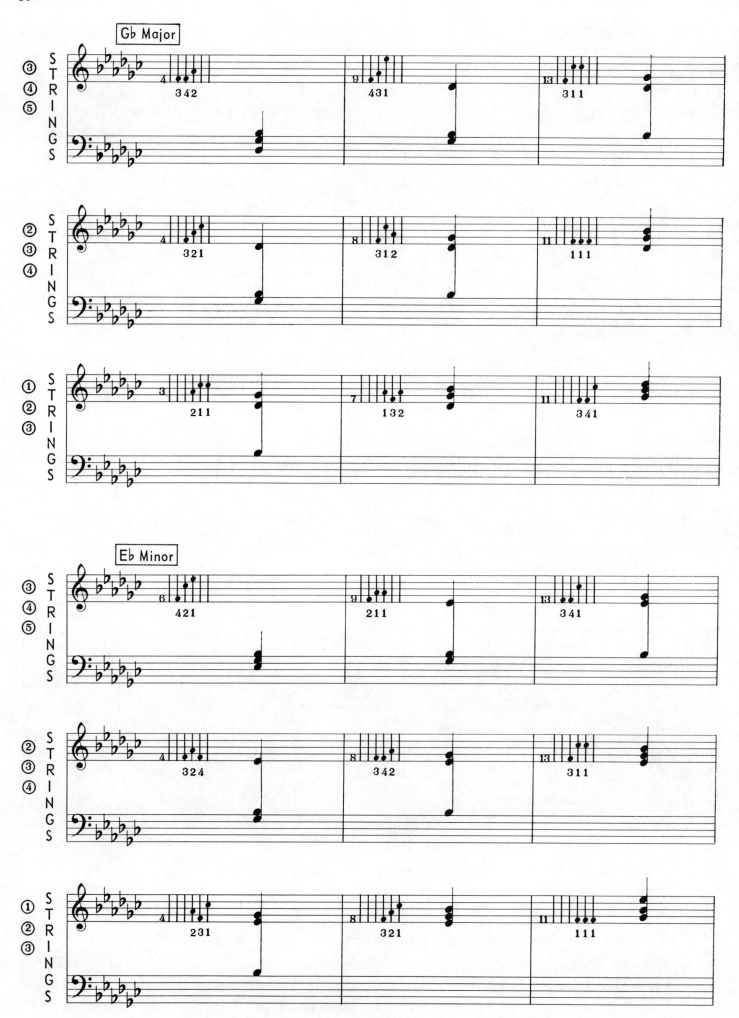

52

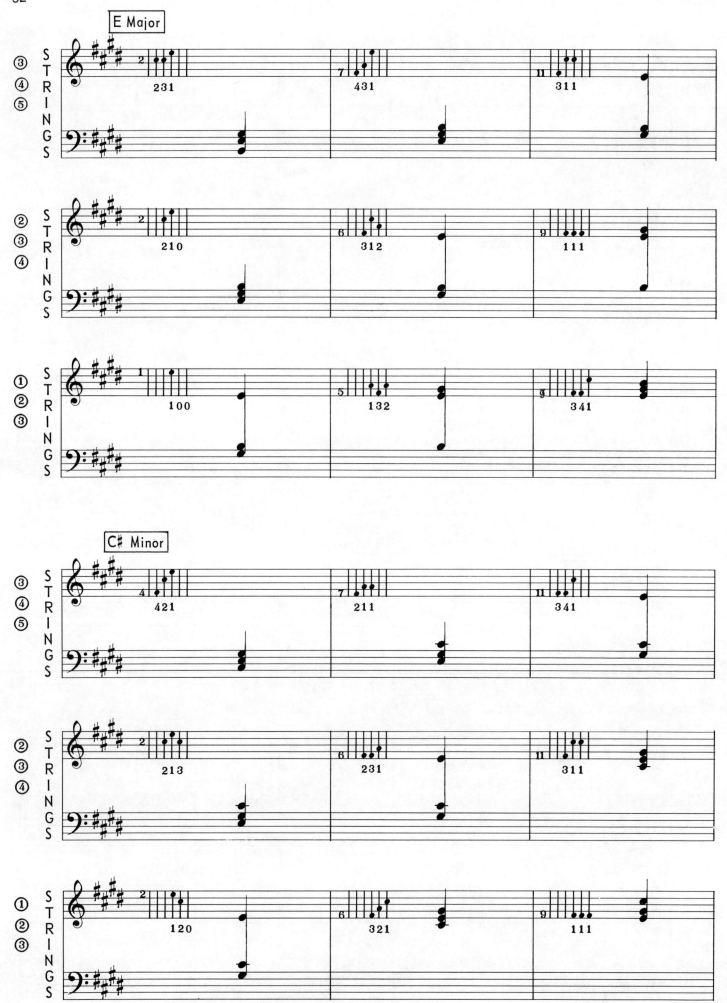

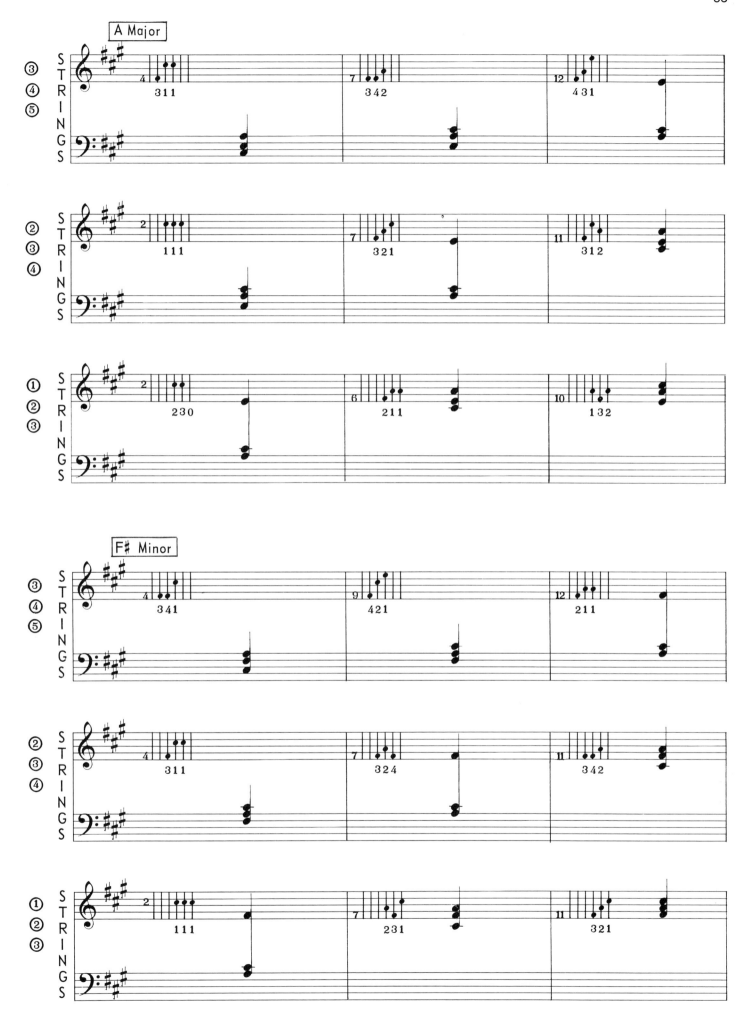

54

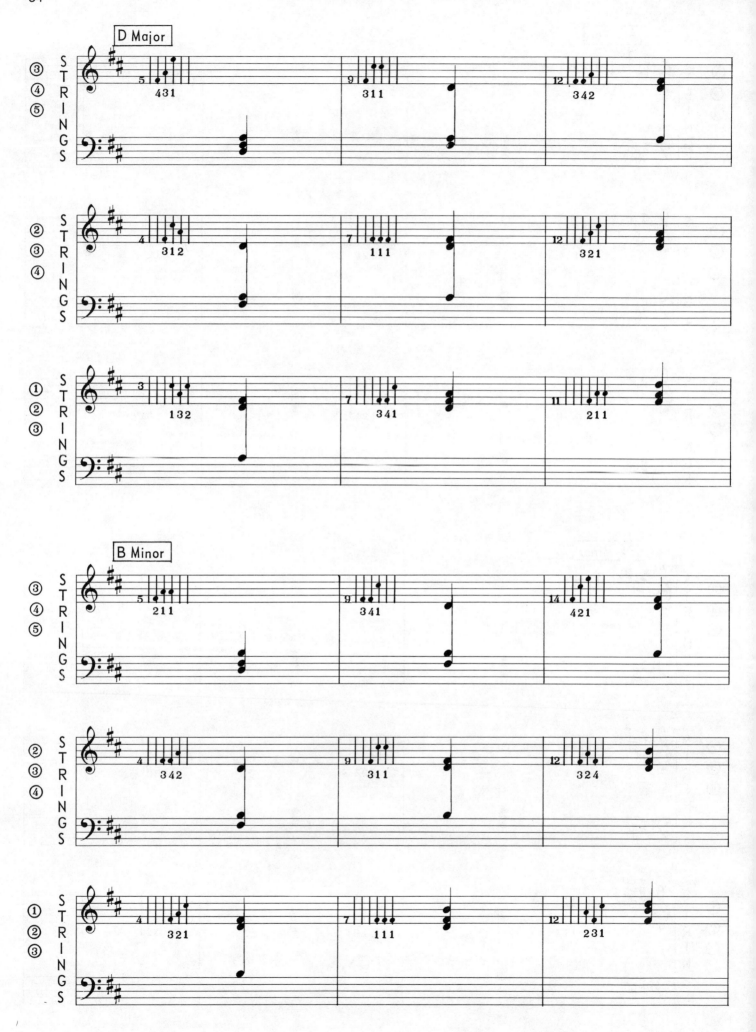

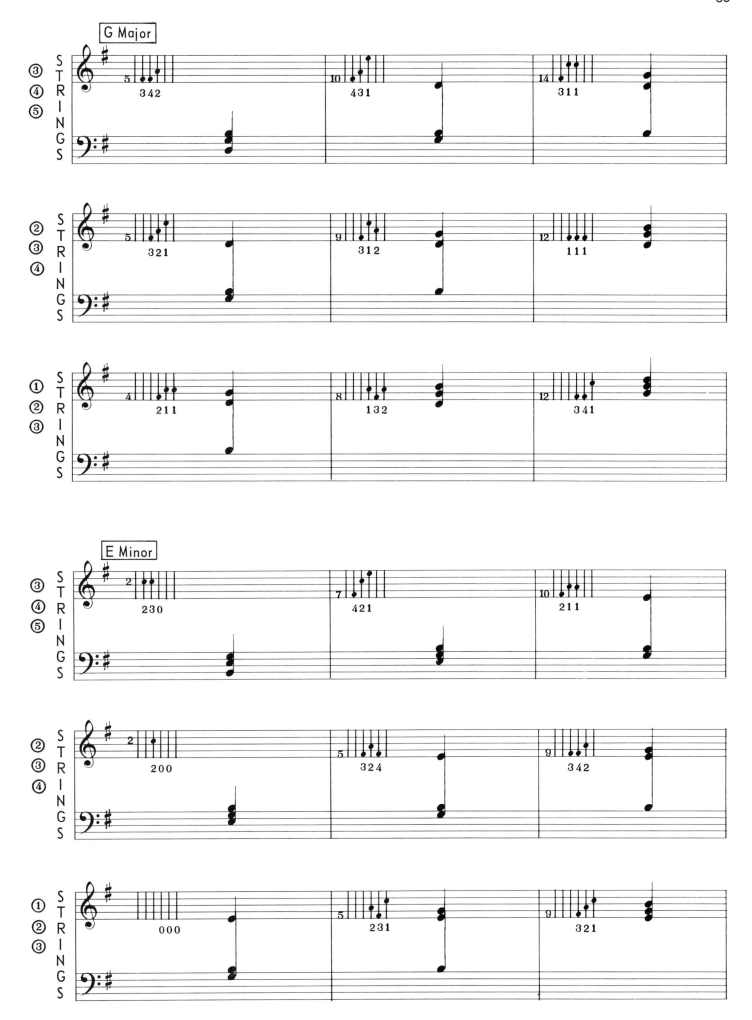

Inversions of Root Position Major and Minor Chords for Rhythm or Accompaniment

When a note other than the root or tonic note is used as the bass note, it should indicated by notation.

Example

There are recommended voicings for these chords and this section will give most common examples.

First Inversions

Example I

(Sixth String)   G major with the third in the bass.

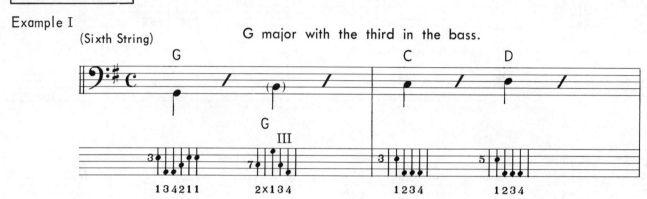

Example II

(Sixth String)   G minor with the minor third in the bass.

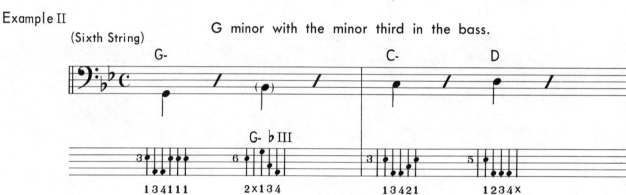

Example III

(Fifth String)   C major with the major third in the bass (C III)

Example IV

(Fifth String)   C minor with the minor third in the bass (C- bIII)

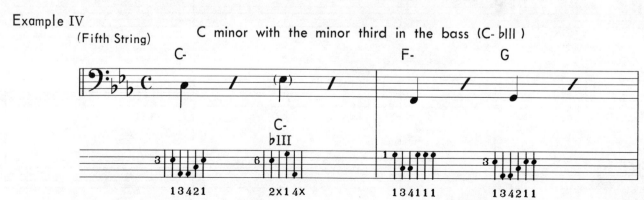

Second Inversions

When voicing the fifth in the bass it is usually better to delete the root note directly above the fifth.

Examples of voicings from basic forms   ①   ②   and   ③

Using form ①

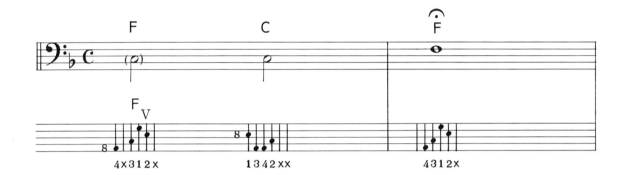

Using form ②

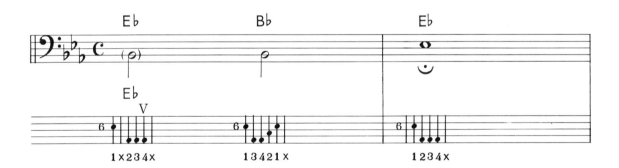

Using form ③

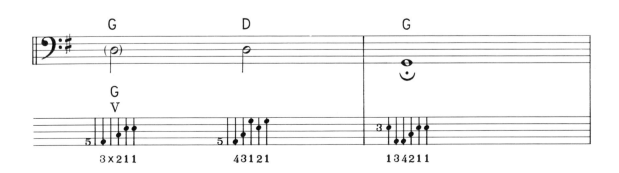

58

Minor chord voicings with the fifth in the bass, forms   and

Using form ① —

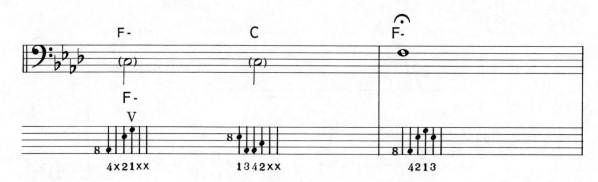

Using form ② —

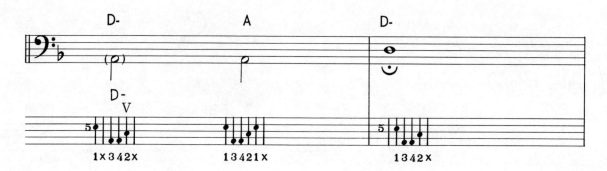

Using form ③ —

There are, of course, many other fingering
possibilities (too numerous to write) but,
these examples will, hopefully, serve as a
basis for your own expansion of ideas.

Major and Minor Arpeggio Studies

These arpeggios should be practiced with alternating picking, using a tempo of approximately ♩=60 to start. Overcoming the tendency to Gliss-Pick (down stroke over two strings) will be the most difficult part of the arpeggio studies.

Striving for evenness of tempo, note value, and consistency of good tone quality will produce performance standards in these exercises. The ability to pick down on one string and up on another is one of the most difficult techniques to acquire on the plectrum guitar; therefore, the concentration in this area is very important.

After the arpeggio forms are memorized and the picking form is established, the practice speed may be increased to ♩=120. Special care should be taken to avoid slurring when the positions shift on the same string.

Naturally, there are many different fingering possibilities, and the player may choose to use fingering other than the ones in these studies. The fingerings in these arpeggios relate closely to the basic forms (2) and (3) major and minor scales which should help with memorization.

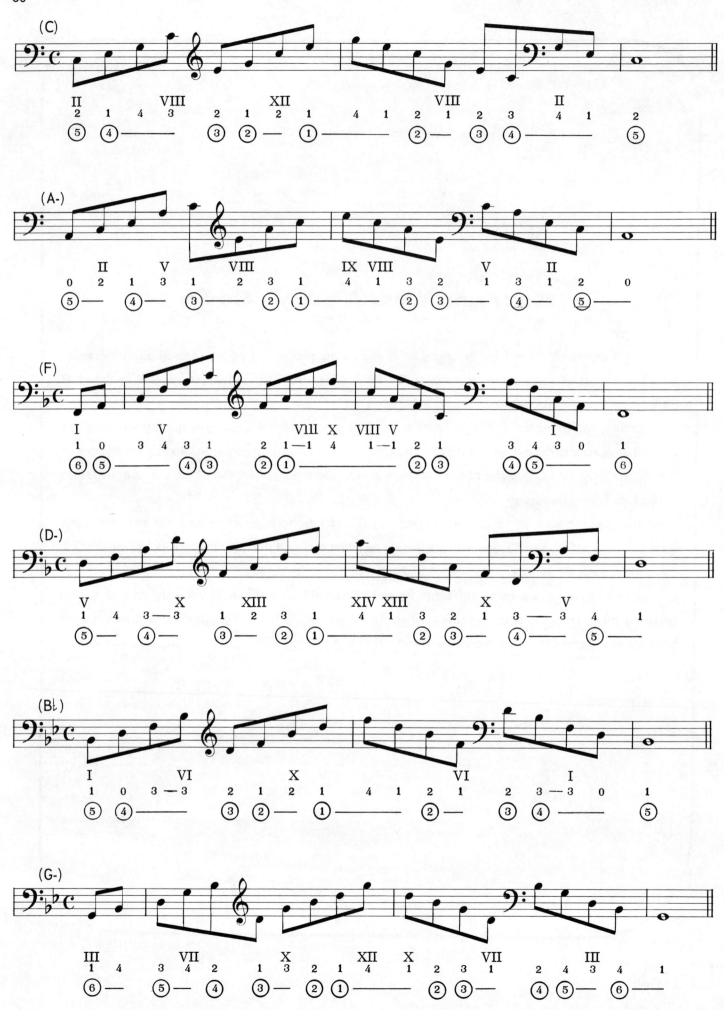

61

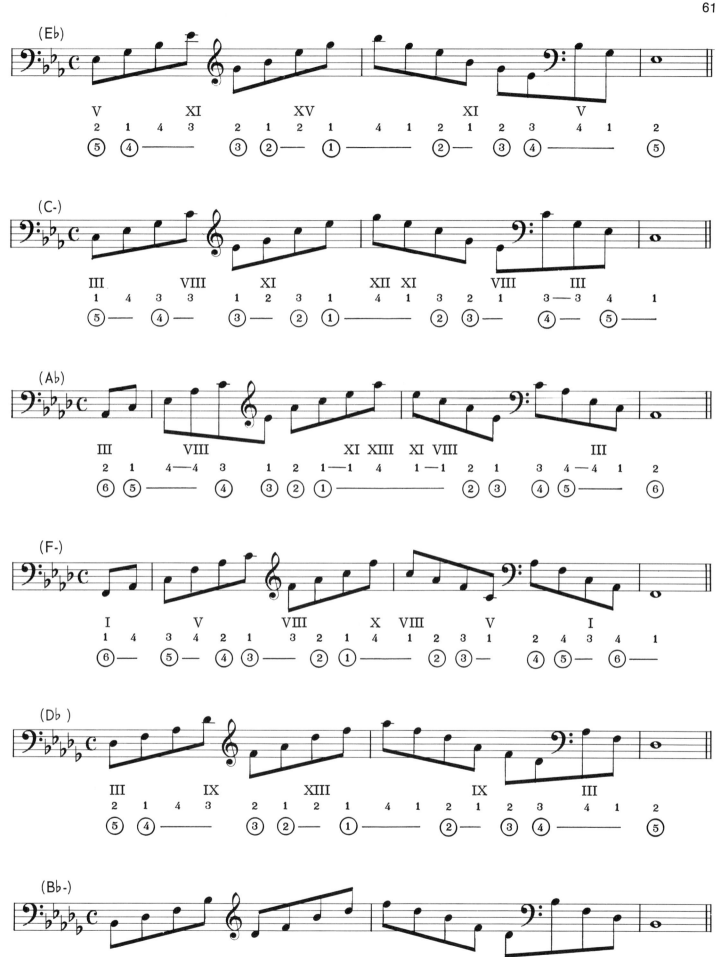

62

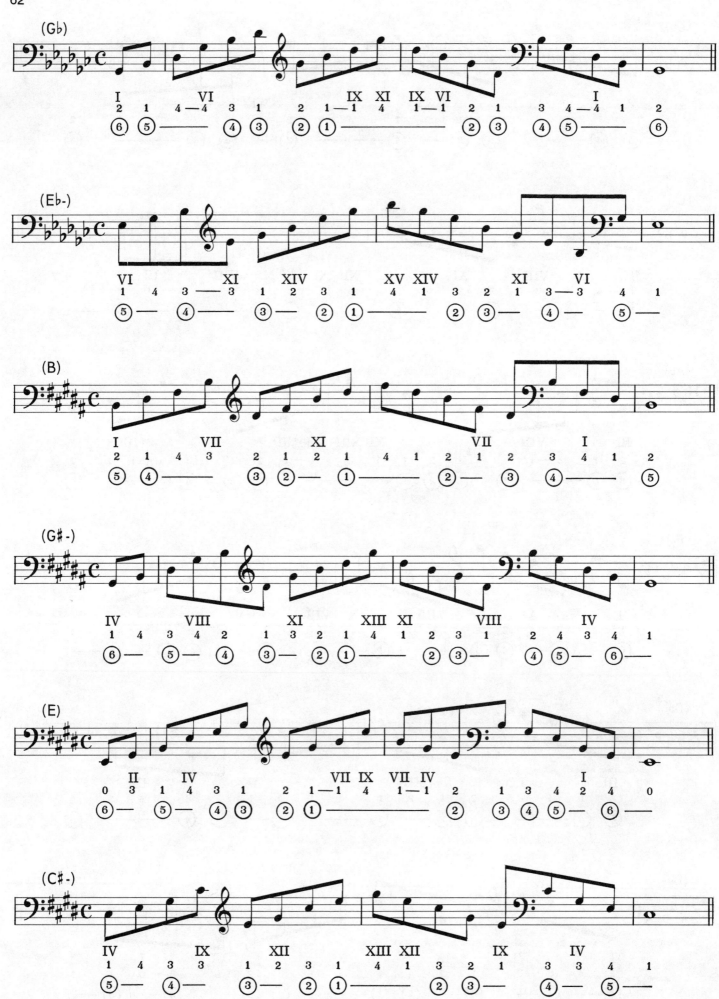

63

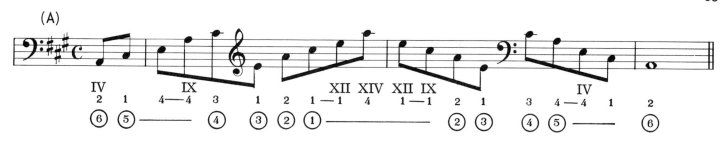

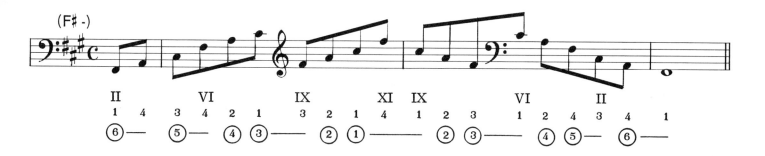

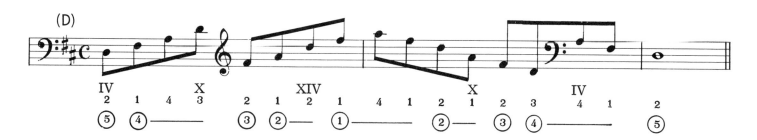

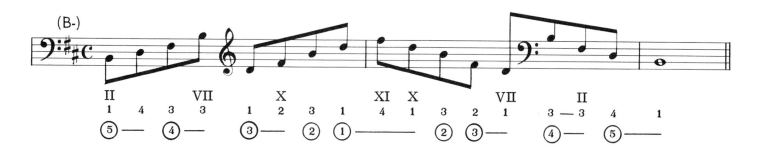

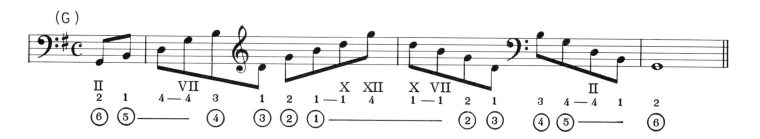

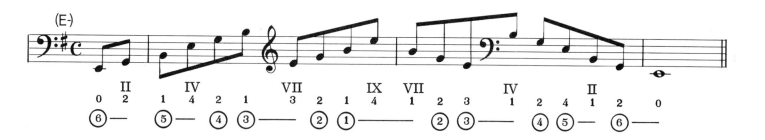

The Major Sixth and Minor Sixth Chords

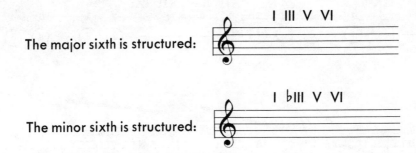

The major sixth is structured: I III V VI

The minor sixth is structured: I ♭III V VI

The major and minor sixth chords are extensions of the major and minor chords. In their pure form (unaltered), the sixth/minor sixth chords *do not resolve*. They are generally used as extensions of major or minor chords in their tonic keys.

It is not in good taste to use a sixth or minor sixth if the melody note is the natural seventh.

Example:

The C6 would not be a good voicing in this case, being a whole step away from the ♮VII (B♮). The (B♮) would make the chord a C Major 7.

Basic Form Major Sixth Chords
(Root Position)

I III V IV   Chord Symbol Example: C6

Open Forms

① open (B6)   ② open (B♭)   ③ open (E6)

31204   1304x   023140

③ open(F6)

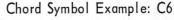

1x032x

Closed Forms

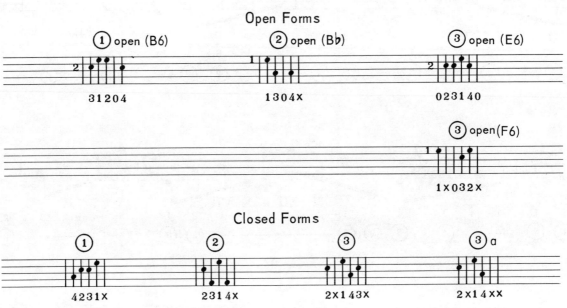

①   ②   ③   ③ a

4231x   2314x   2x143x   2x14xx

NOTE: The fifth (V) in Form 1 closed is omitted.

Form ② can be fingered more easily by placing the 3rd and 4th fingers first and letting the hand roll back until 1st and 2nd fingers note comfortably. Do not try to keep the thumb behind the neck.

Form ③ a will be used in a rhythm exercise with major sevenths.

66

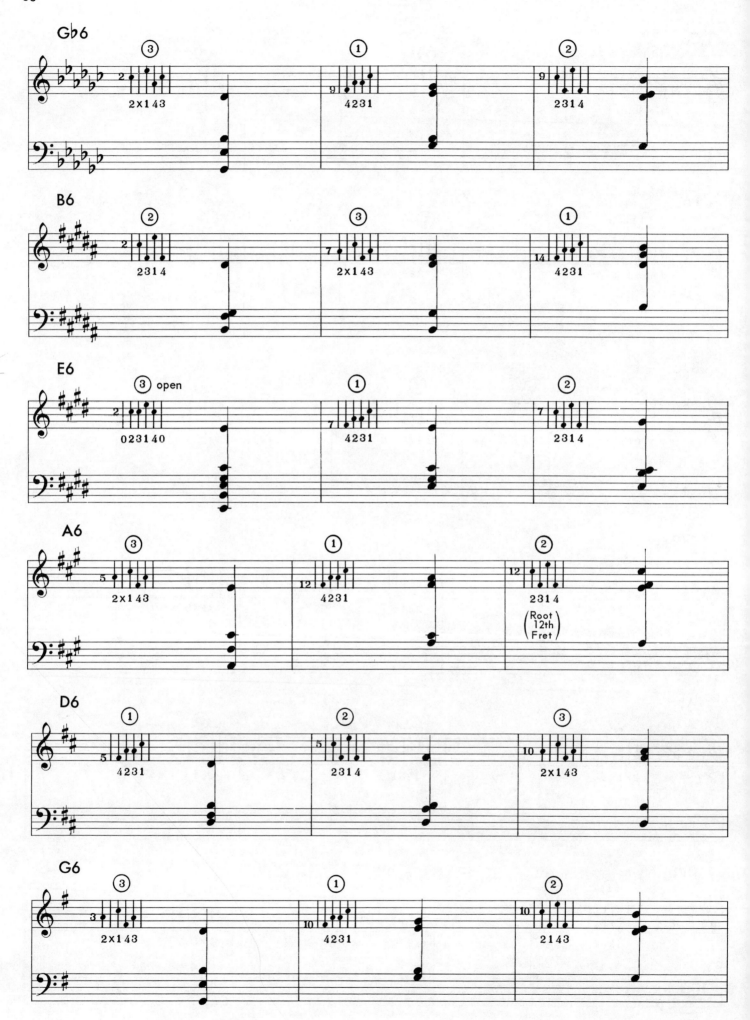

Write In FRET NUMBER For The Root Notes Of The Basic Form
Major Sixth Chords (All Keys)

		Fret No.		Fret No.		Fret No.
C6	①	3	②	3	③	8
F6	③	open ——	①	——	②	——
B♭6	②	open ——	③	——	①	——
E♭6	①	——	②	——	③	——
A♭6	③	——	①	——	②	——
D♭6	①	——	②	——	③	——
G♭6	③	——	①	——	②	——
B6	①	open ——	②	——	③	——
E6	③	open ——	①	——	②	——
A6	③	——	①	——	②	——
D6	①	——	②	——	③	——
G6	③	——	①	——	②	——

THIS SEQUENCE SHOULD BE MEMORIZED.

Root Position Inversions of the Major Sixth Chords

These Inversions of the Basic Forms would be used mostly for rhythm and accompaniment. A Root Inversion, when desired, should be indicated by notation as shown in the following exercises:

69

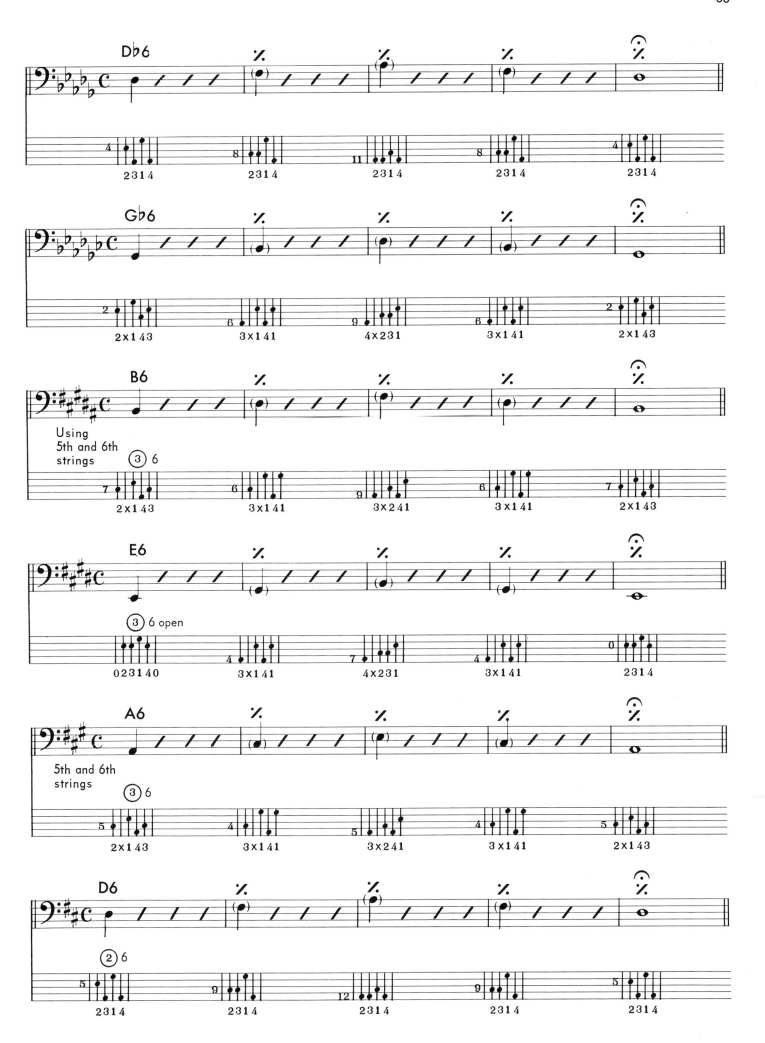

Like the major and minor chords, these inversions could be called:
1st Inversion and 2nd Inversion
(III in the bass) (V in the bass)

They could also be indicated with a chord symbol as follows:

$$G^6_{III} \quad \text{or} \quad G^6_V$$

(third in bass)   (fifth in bass)

Some examples of phrases using inversions of the Major Sixth Chords.

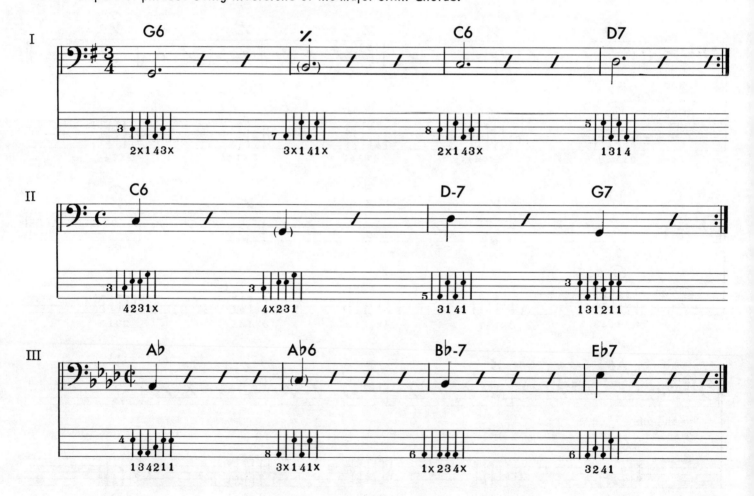

Example of a descending diatonic bass line using Major 6th and Dominant 7th inversions.

Alteration of the Major Sixth Chord
(Major Sixth Flat Five)

I III ♭V VI   Chord Symbol Example: C6♭5

Because of the basic form ① closed having the five omitted, only basic forms ② and ③ will be used.

OPEN FORMS

(Avoid picking 5th and 1st strings)

CLOSED FORMS

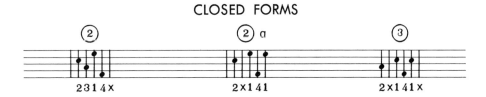

The basic resolution of a major sixth flat five chord is to a dominant seventh chord ½ step lower.
Example B♭6♭5 ⟶ A7

Because of the modal quality of the 6♭5, the progressions will resolve to minor chord, as shown in the key signatures.

The following examples show the 6♭5 chords resolving ½ step lower to the closest, root position, dominant seventh chord. The dominant sevenths would usually resolve then, to a IV minor.

C6♭5 to B7 to E -

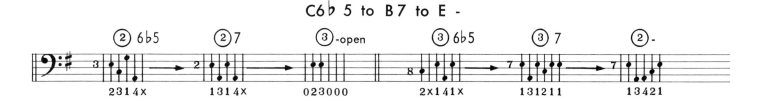

F6♭5 to E7 to A—

B♭6♭5 to A7 to D-

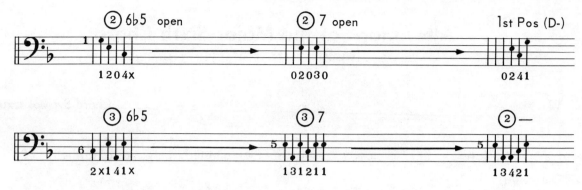

E♭6♭5 to D7 to G-

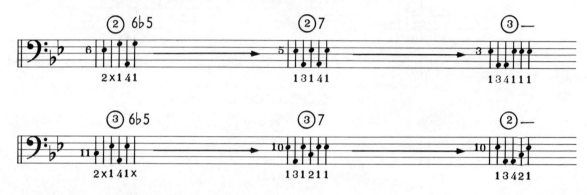

A♭6♭5 to G7 to C-

(Use similiar fingerings for chord forms)

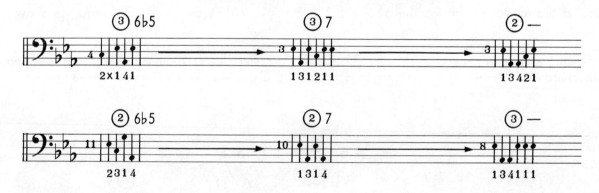

D♭6♭5 to C7 to F-

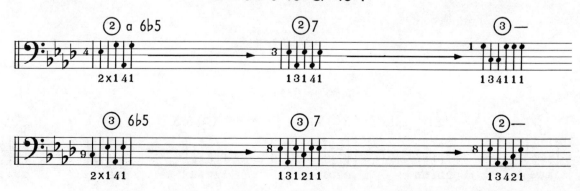

73

G♭6♭5 to F7 to B♭-

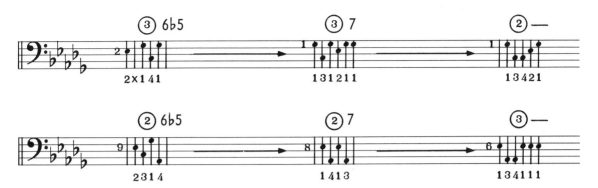

C♭6♭5 to B♭7 to E♭-

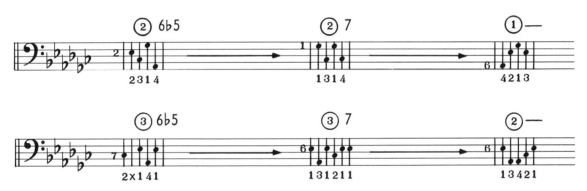

E6♭5 to D♯7 to G♯-

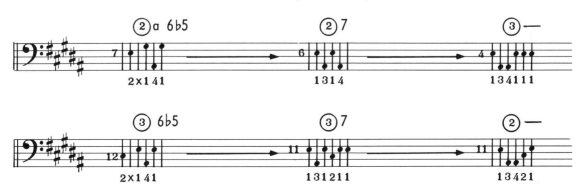

74

A6♭5 to G♯7 to C♯-

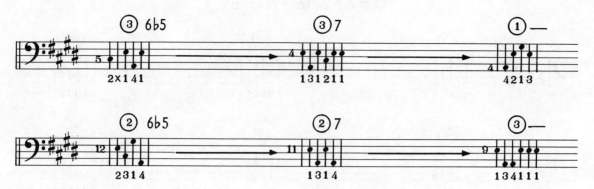

D6♭5 to C♯7 to F♯-

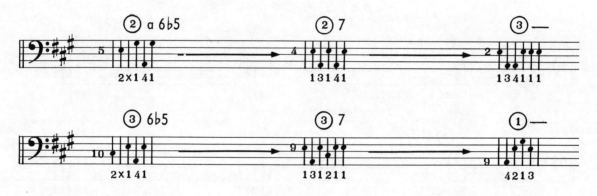

G6♭5 to F♯7 to B-

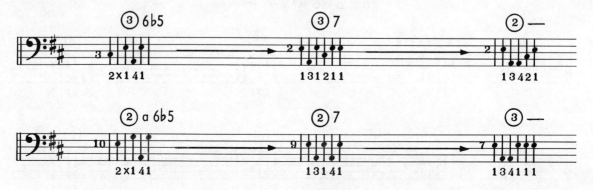

THE MINOR SIXTH CHORDS

I ♭III V VI

Chord Symbol Example: C-6

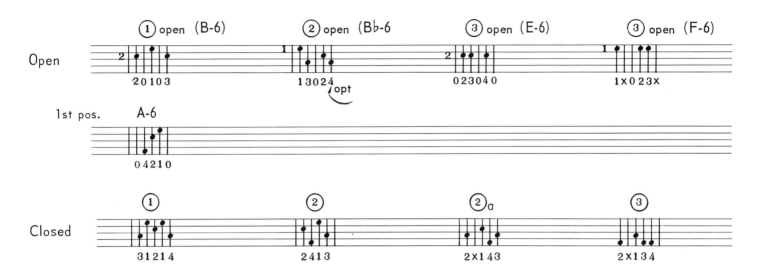

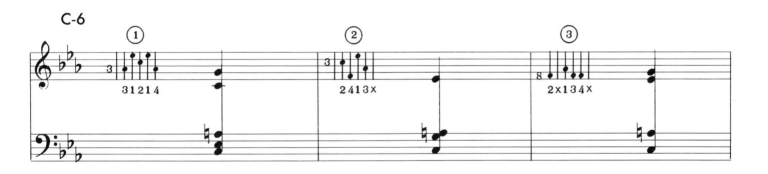

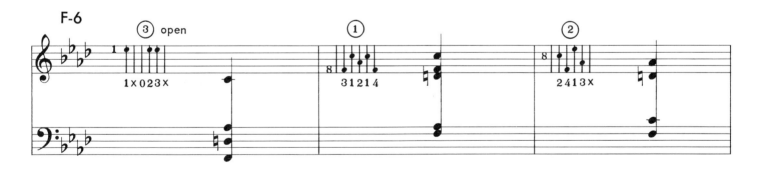

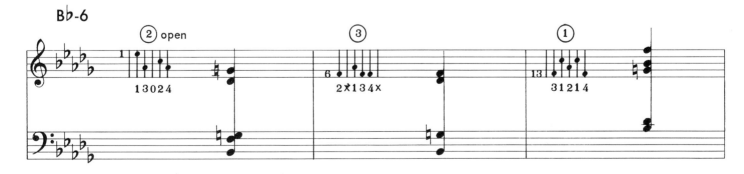

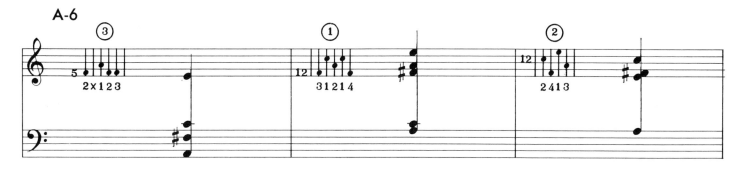

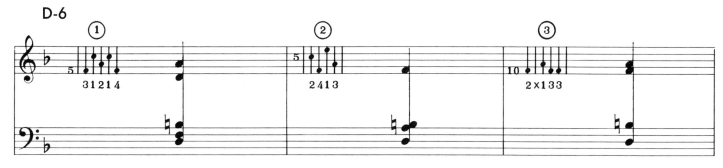

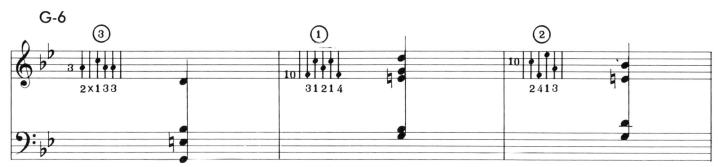

MEMORIZE:

C-6	①	②	③
F-6	③ open	①	②
B♭-6	② open	③	①
E♭-6	①	②	③
G♯-6	③	①	②
C♯-6	①	②	③
F♯-6	③	①	②
B-6	②	③	①
E-6	③ open	①	②
A-6	③	①	②
D-6	①	②	③
G-6	③	①	②

Root Position Inversions of the Minor Sixth Chords
(used mostly for rhythm and accompaniment)

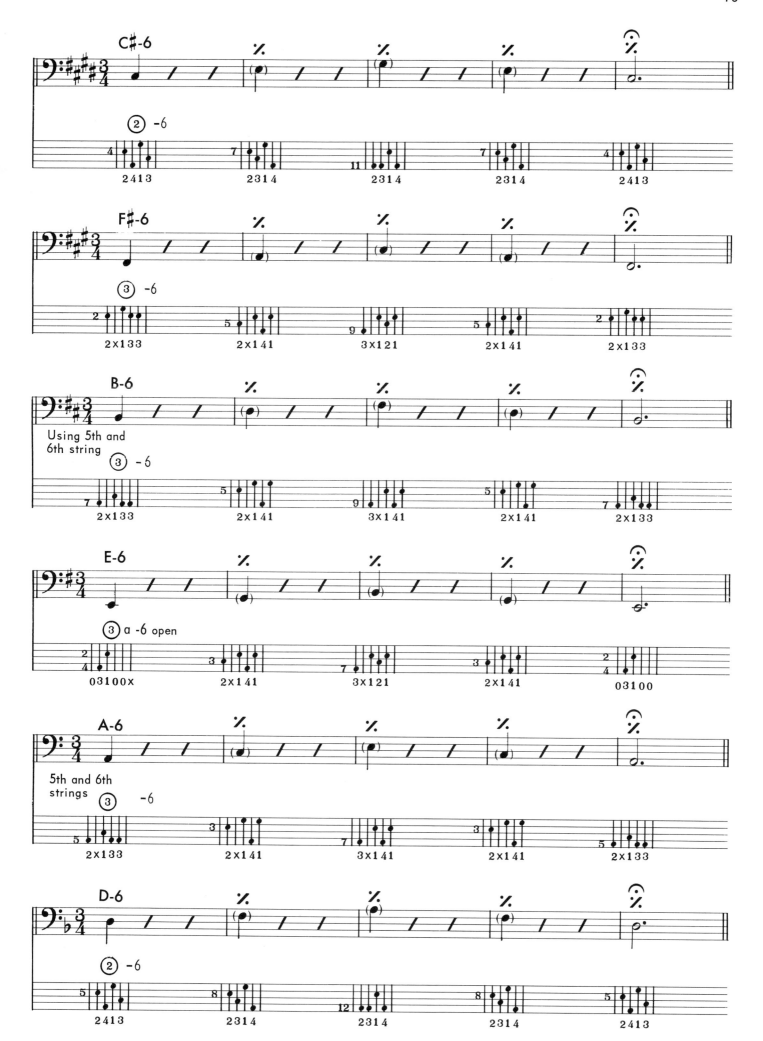

Like the major sixth, the minor sixth inversions could be called the   1st   or   2nd inversion.

(♭III in bass) (V in bass)

The 3rd inversion (VI in the bass) is not commonly used. The inversions may also be indicated by the chord symbols: C-$^6_{♭III}$ C-$^6_{V}$

Some examples of phrases using inversions of the minor sixth chords:

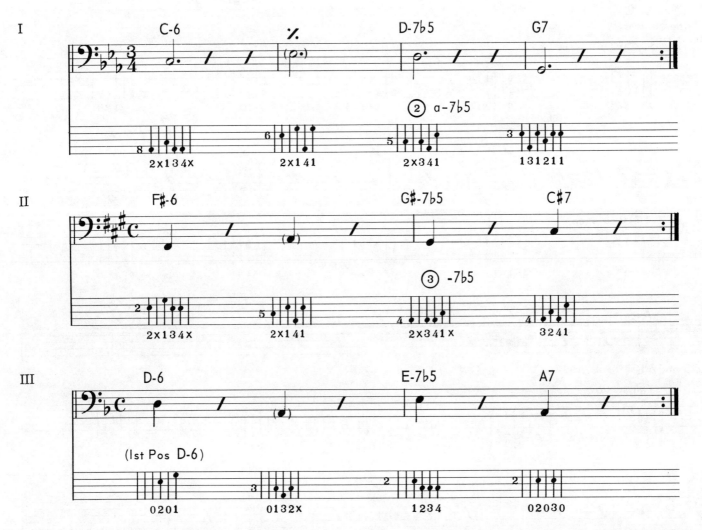

It is interesting to note at this point that the alteration of the minor sixth (lowered V), would give us a diminished seventh chord. Diminished sevenths (minor third intervals) will be taken up thoroughly in Part II.

Upper Structure Inversions of the Minor Sixth (Dominant Ninth) Chords

The upper structure of a dominant ninth chord is the same tonal arrangement as the minor sixth chord and its inversions. An easy association can be made by thinking of a minor sixth chord (or inversion) as the upper structure of a Dom 9th chord a fourth step above.

Example:

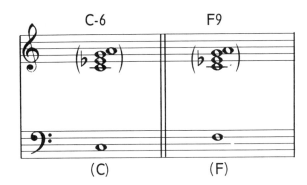

As you notice, the top notes (upper structure) are identical in both chords.

C-6/F9 (Tonic notes circled)

82

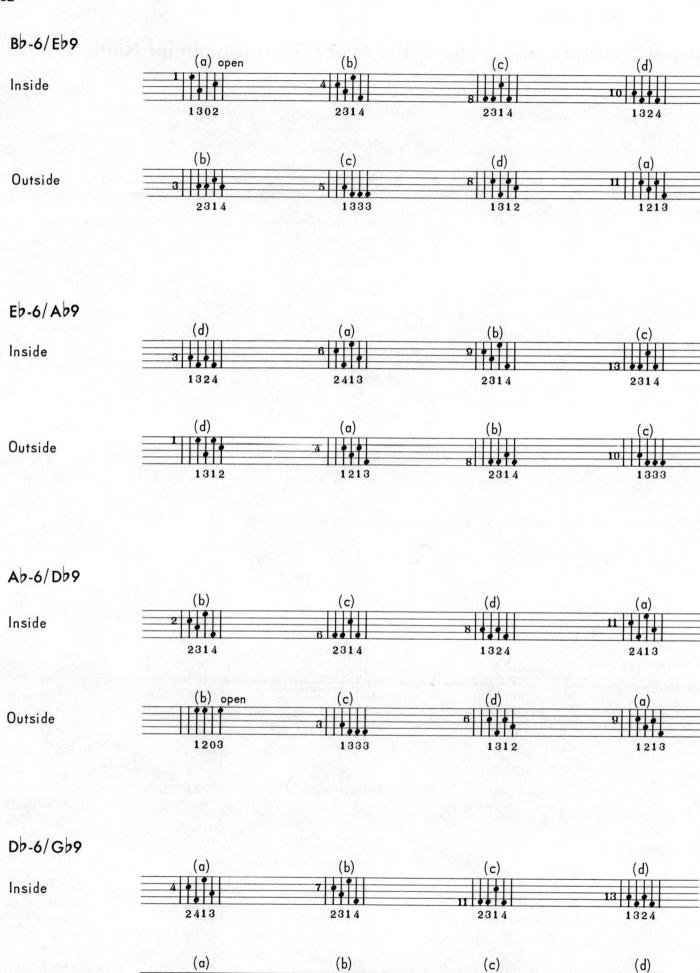

F#-6/B9

Inside

Outside

B-6/E9

Inside

Outside

E-6/A9

Inside

Outside

A-6/D9

Inside

Outside

D-6/G9

Inside

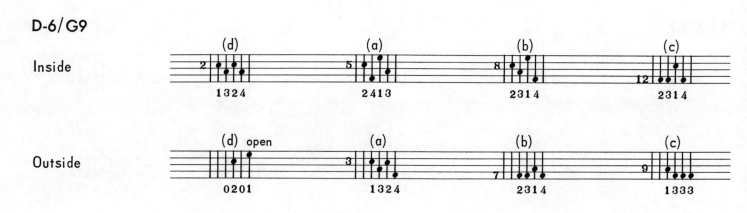

Outside

G-6/C9

Inside

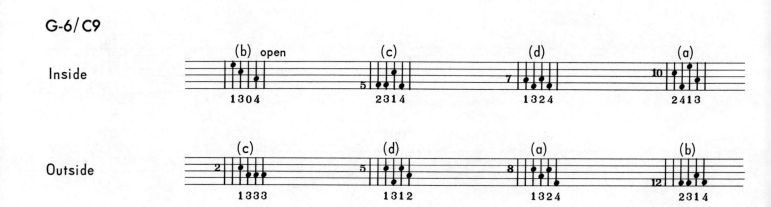

Outside

Application of Inversions

Discretion is required on the part of the player to avoid undesirable chord voicings. Even though the notation is correct, the pitch, in which some of these inversions could be used, could produce an unpleasant musical voicing. Take as an example form (c) G-6/C9. If the player were to use this inversion for the upper structure of a C chord, the bottom note (in this example) D, which being the 9th of a C chord, would be only one whole tone away from the bass note C. This is considered to be a musically bad voicing in the bass clef, and being considered as such, should be avoided by the guitarist.

The sequence and rotation patterns of these forms should be memorized.

	Inside					→	**Outside**				
C–6 / F9	(a)		(b)	(c)	(d)	→	(a)		(b)	(c)	(d)
F–6 / B♭9	(c)		(d)	(a)	(b)	→	(c)	open	(d)	(a)	(b)
B♭–6 / E♭9	(a)	open	(b)	(c)	(d)	→	(b)		(c)	(d)	(a)
E♭–6 / A♭9	(d)		(a)	(b)	(c)	→	(d)		(a)	(b)	(c)
A♭–6 / D♭9	(b)		(c)	(d)	(a)	→	(b)	open	(c)	(d)	(a)
D♭–6 / G♭9	(a)		(b)	(c)	(d)	→	(a)		(b)	(c)	(d)
F#–6 / B9	(c)		(d)	(a)	(b)	→	(c)		(d)	(a)	(b)
B–6 / E9	(a)		(b)	(c)	(d)	→	(a)	open	(b)	(c)	(d)
E–6 / A9	(c)	open	(d)	(a)	(b)	→	(d)		(a)	(b)	(c)
A–6 / D9	(b)		(c)	(d)	(a)	→	(b)		(c)	(d)	(a)
D–6 / G9	(d)		(a)	(b)	(c)	→	(d)	open	(a)	(b)	(c)
G–6 / C9	(b)	open	(c)	(d)	(a)	→	(c)		(d)	(a)	(b)

Introduction to the
Seventh Chords

There are four different types of seventh chords. The dominant seventh (I III V ^{b}VII), the minor seventh (I ^{b}III V ^{b}VII), the major seventh (I III V $\natural$VII) and the minor with a natural seventh (I ^{b}III V $\natural$VII).

The dom 7th and the min 7th usually resolve to a fourth.

$$\text{Ex.} \quad \text{C7} \longrightarrow \text{F}$$
$$\text{Ex.} \quad \text{C–7} \longrightarrow \text{F7} \longrightarrow \text{B}b$$

The maj 7 and the min $\natural$7 usually resolve to a $\underline{\text{I}}$ 6 or $\underline{\text{I}}$ –6

$$\text{Ex.} \quad \text{C maj 7} \longrightarrow \text{C6}$$
$$\text{Ex.} \quad \text{C–} \natural7 \longrightarrow \text{C–6}$$

The term 'minor' when used to depict a chord or chord symbol, refers strictly to the third of the chord, not to the seventh.

$$\text{Ex.} \quad \text{C minor seventh} = \text{C–7 (I } ^b\text{III} \quad \text{V} ^b\text{VII)}$$

Because of the resolutions to other chords, some chord forms may be abbreviated, expecially the min 7th and the maj 7, to help in making these changes smoothly and with a minimum amount of effort. This consideration is very important when playing a fast accompaniment tempo or a rapid chordal passage.

As an example, a rhythmical passage such as this:

could be played easily at any tempo by reducing the number of notes in the chord to two notes each, the *third* and the *seventh*.

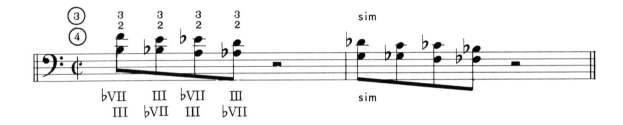

When progressing in fourth steps, such as the above example, note that the thirds resolve to sevenths and the sevenths resolve to thirds when moved chromatically down.

This same principal will apply to many other types of chords where the bass or roots are moving in fourths. The upper structures will move chromatically.

THE BASIC FORM DOMINANT SEVENTH CHORDS
(Root Position)

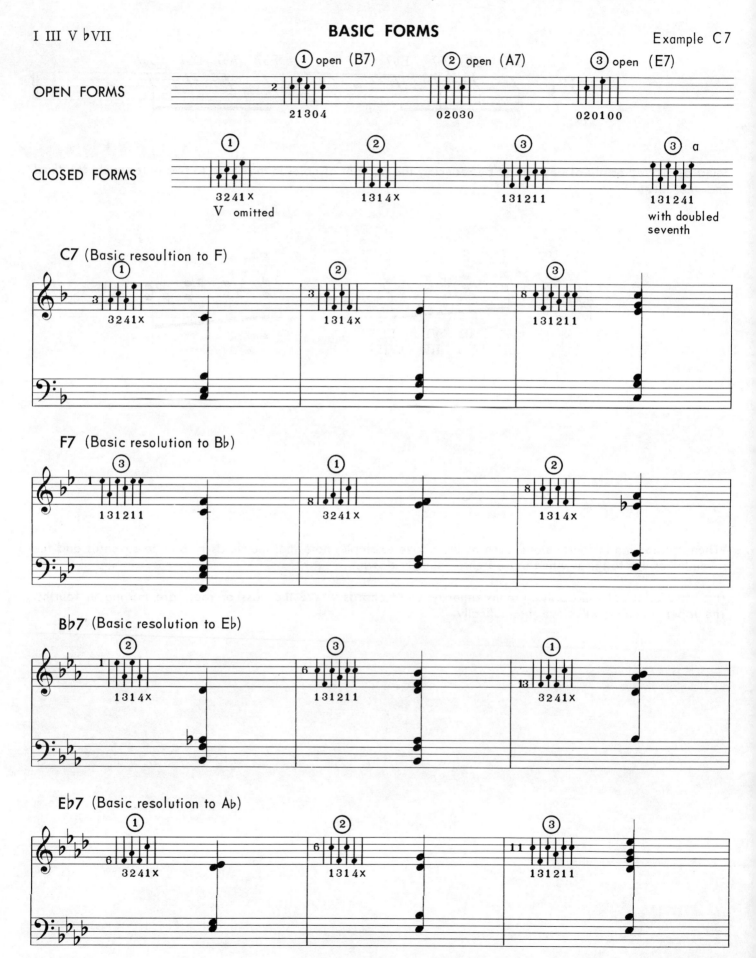

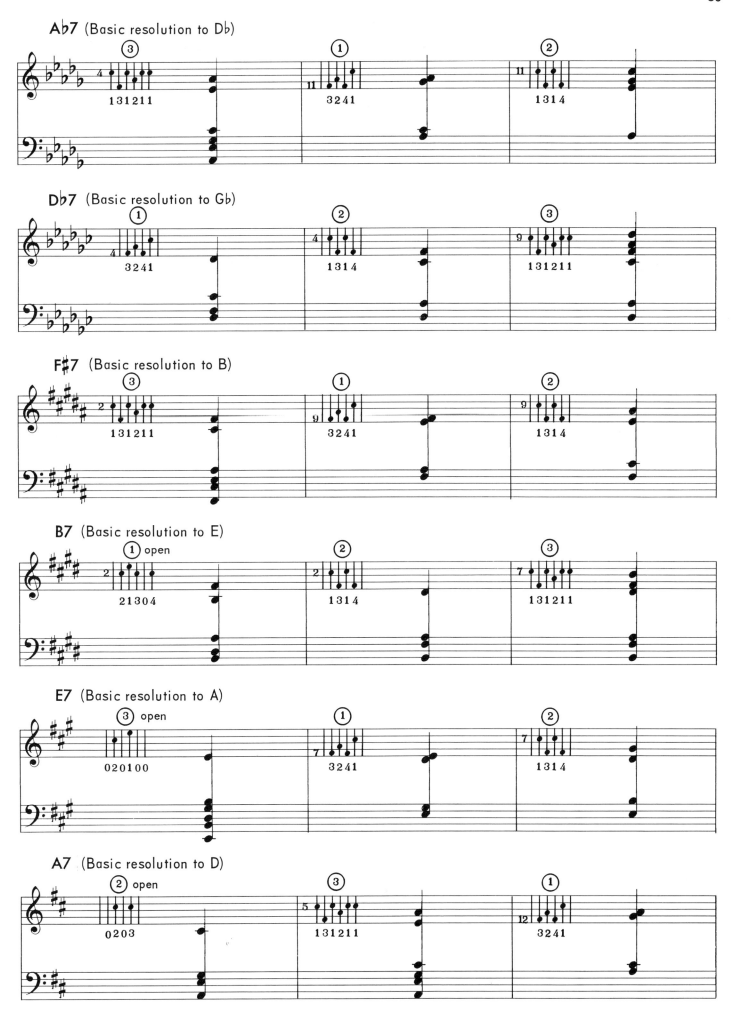

D7 (Basic resolution to G)

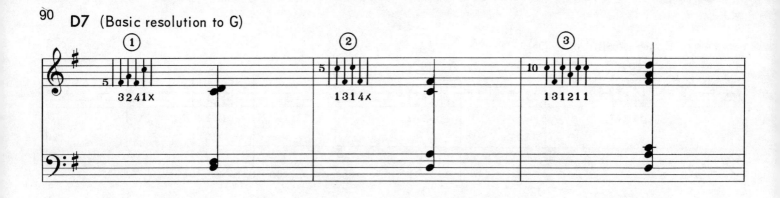

G7 (Basic resolution to C)

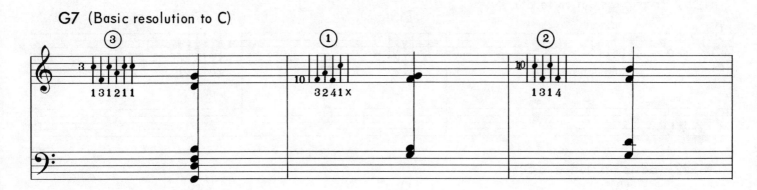

WRITE IN THE *POSITION NUMBERS* (The Fret No. on which the *Index Finger* is placed) FOR THE FOLLOWING.

C7	① open	I	②	III	③	VIII
F7	③	—	①	—	②	—
Bb7	②	—	③	—	①	—
Eb7	①	—	②	—	③	—
Ab7	③	—	①	—	②	—
Db7	①	—	②	—	③	—
F#7	③	—	①	—	②	—
B7	① open	—	②	—	③	—
E7	③ open	—	①	—	②	—
A7	② open	—	③	—	①	—
D7	①	—	②	—	③	—
G7	③	—	①	—	②	—

This sequence should be memorized.

Root Inversions of the Dominant Seventh Chords
(used mostly for rhythm and accompaniment)

Example I

Voicing the seventh chords with the *third* in the bass.

Root on the ⑤ string.

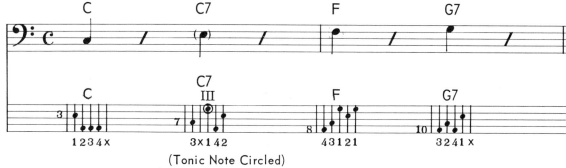

(Tonic Note Circled)

Root on the ⑥ string.

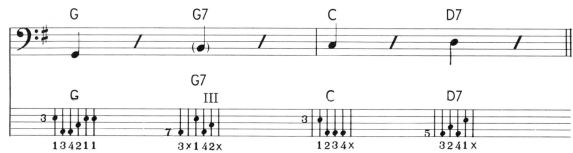

Example II

Voicing the seventh chords with the *flat seventh* in the bass. The most common bass line progression is for the flat seventh to resolve to IV major with the third in the bass.

Root on the ⑤ string.

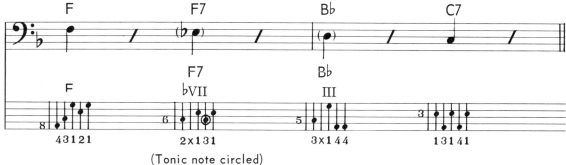

(Tonic note circled)

Root on the ⑥ string.

You will notice, as on all of the examples of root inversions, that care has been taken in the chord forms to avoid duplication of the bass notes in the upper structure of the chord.

Upper Structure Inversions of the Dominant Seventh Chords

The voicings of the chords used in these inversions would be called 'OPEN' voicings. That is to say that the notes are not arranged in perfect vertical spacing. Here is an example of a 'C7' chord with the notes arranged in perfect spacing down from 'C' on the top.

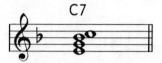

To finger this exact notation would be very difficult on the guitar, as shown in this diagram:
(a span of six frets)

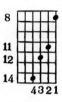

As you can see, this is not a practical chord form to use. The method used to open these vertical spacings, making a much more practical fingering, is called the *DROP TONE SYSTEM*. We simply drop the *SECOND TONE FROM THE TOP* one octave lower.

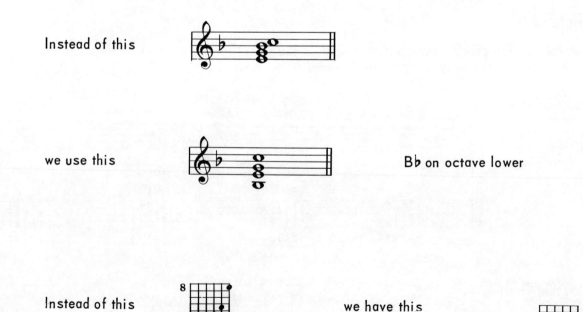

Which, as you see, is a much more practical and easier fingering.
This sequence, especially the rotation pattern of these forms, should be memorized.

C7 (Tonic notes are circled)

Inside

Outside

F7

Inside

Outside

B♭7

Inside

Outside

E♭7

Inside

Outside

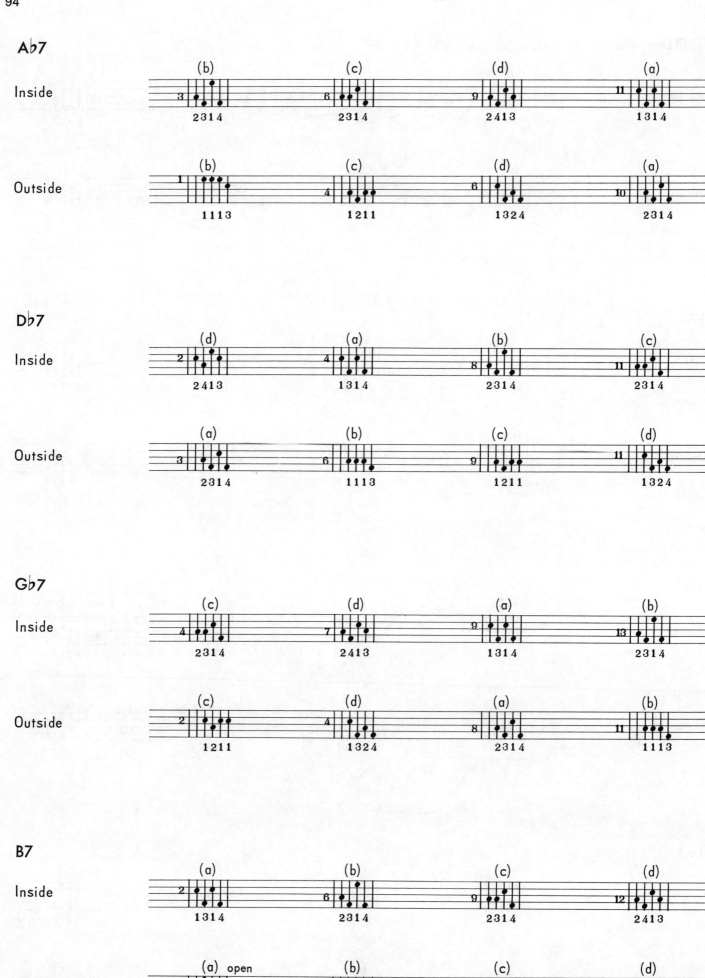

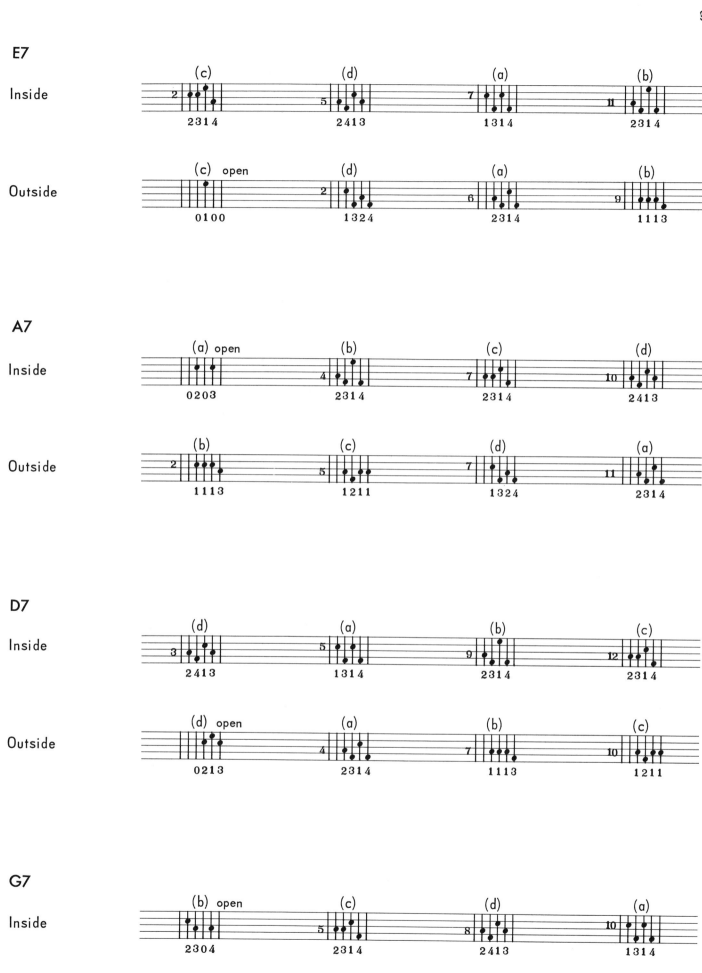

Memorize:

	Inside						**Outside**			
C7	(a)		(b)	(c)	(d)	→	(a)		(b)	(c)	(d)
F7	(c)		(d)	(a)	(b)	→	(c)		(d)	(a)	(b)
B^{b}7	(a)		(b)	(c)	(d)	→	(b)		(c)	(d)	(a)
E^{b}7	(c)	open	(d)	(a)	(b)	→	(d)		(a)	(b)	(c)
A^{b}7	(b)		(c)	(d)	(a)	→	(b)		(c)	(d)	(a)
D^{b}7	(d)		(a)	(b)	(c)	→	(a)		(b)	(c)	(d)
G^{b}7	(c)		(d)	(a)	(b)	→	(c)		(d)	(a)	(b)
B 7	(a)		(b)	(c)	(d)	→	(a)	open	(b)	(c)	(d)
E7	(c)		(d)	(a)	(b)	→	(c)	open	(d)	(a)	(b)
A7	(a)	open	(b)	(c)	(d)	→	(b)		(c)	(d)	(a)
D7	(d)		(a)	(b)	(c)	→	(d)	open	(a)	(b)	(c)
G7	(b)	open	(c)	(d)	(a)	→	(b)	open	(c)	(d)	(a)

Alterations of the Dominant Seventh Chords

The Seventh Flat Five   I   III♭V   ♭VII   Chord Symbol Example: C7(♭5)

BASIC FORMS

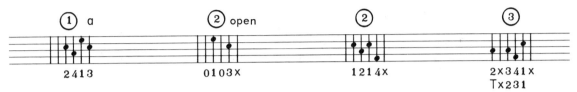

Form ①a would be used more as the upper structure of a 7♭5 chord and can be named by the notes on the 1st or 2nd string. Forms ② open, ② and ③ would be used more for rhythm and accompaniment. The seven flat five is a polytonic chord. As example, a C7 ♭5 has the identical notes as a G♭7♭5. As in all of the non-inverted chords, the bass note (root) determines the chord name. The polytonic relationship can be determined by recognizing the flat five (G♭ is the flat five of C, and C is the flat five of G♭) or looking directly across the chord cycle chart. (2 examples shown below)

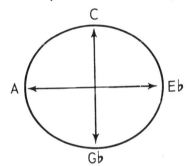

These chords *should not be substituted* however, and should be named by the bass note.

A (7 ♭ 5) chord can resolve in two ways basically:

1. to a fourth step   Example: (C7 ♭ 5 ⟶ F)

2. to a half step lower   Example   (B♭7♭ 5 ⟶ A)

J. S. Part I

The Augmented Seventh

I III+V ♭VII

Chord Symbol Example C+7
C7(+5)

BASIC FORMS

* ① (Root omitted)   ②   ③

1 2 1 1 x   1 4 1 3 x   1 x 2 3 4 x

*Circle indicates the location of the root of that chord form. This form should be avoided in the lower positions if possible.

Form ② is not a common voicing for the aug 7th chord but could be used well if the melody were on the third.

Example

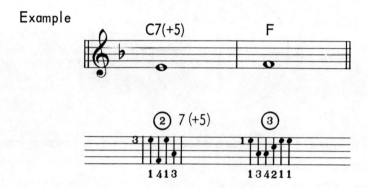

② 7 (+5)   ③

1 4 1 3   1 3 4 2 1 1

The basic resolution of an aug 7th chord is a fourth step.

Example

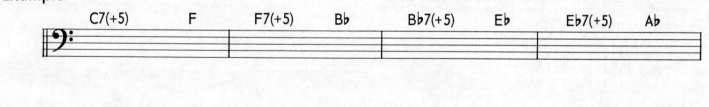

C7(+5)   F   F7(+5)   B♭   B♭7(+5)   E♭   E♭7(+5)   A♭

A♭7(+5)   D♭   D♭7(+5)   G♭   F♯7(+5)   B   B7(+5)   E   E7(+5)   A

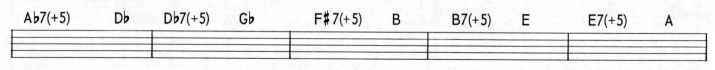

A7(+5)   D   D7(+5)   G   G7(+5)   C

THE BASIC FORM MINOR SEVENTH CHORDS
(Root Position)

I bIII V bVII   Chord Symbol Example C-7

The basic resolution of a min 7th chord is to IV$_7$.

BASIC FORMS

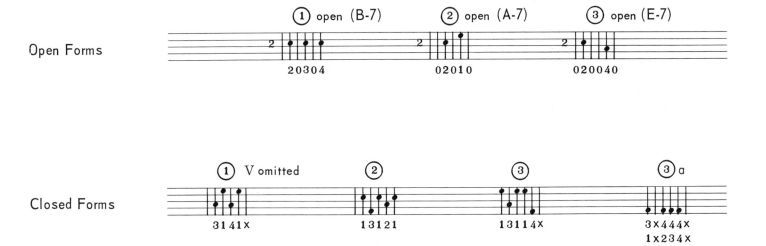

Open Forms

① open (B-7)   ② open (A-7)   ③ open (E-7)
20304   02010   020040

Closed Forms

① V omitted   ②   ③   ③a
31 41x   13121   13114x   3x444x
                                              1x234x

Using the fourth finger bar (basic form ③ a-7) because of the frequent use of the basic form ③ a min 7th and the usual resolution of the ③ a min 7th to a ① dom 7 (ex. C-7 ➤ F7) the fourth finger bar makes this commonly used chord progression much easier for the plectrum guitarist. (Fourth finger bar is not generally recommended for the classic guitar.)

Acquiring the ability to apply pressure with the fourth finger in a way that the first joint of the finger remains relaxed (collapses with pressure) is the hardest part of the fourth finger bar. It is, however, the only way that the fourth finger can be barred and still keep the palm of the hand close to the neck.

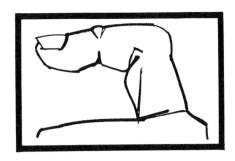

C-7 (Basic Resolution to F7)

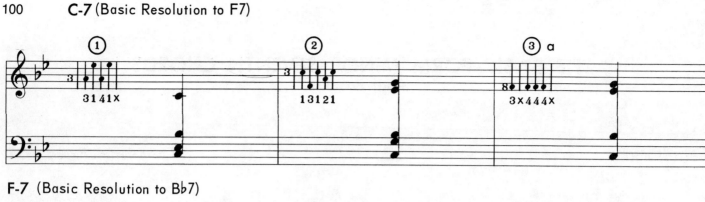

F-7 (Basic Resolution to Bb7)

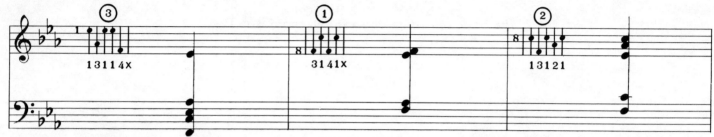

Bb-7 (Basic Resolution to Eb7)

Eb-7 (Basic Resolution to Ab7)

Ab-7 (Basic Resolution to Db7)

C#-7 (Basic Resolution to F#7)

Note the major triads in the upper structure of forms ② and ③a. These triads may be inverted (see maj triad inversions pg. 61) to give chodal patterns or arpeggiated as a nucleous for a melodic phrase.

Memorize:

C–7	①	②	③ a
F–7	③	①	②
B♭–7	②	③ a	①
E♭–7	①	②	③ a
A♭–7	③ a	①	②
C#–7	①	②	③ a
F#–7	③	①	②
B–7	① open	②	③ a
E–7	③ open	①	②
A–7	② open	③ a	①
D–7	①	②	③ a
G–7	③ a	①	②

Exercises for Min 7th to 7th Progressions

Excercise

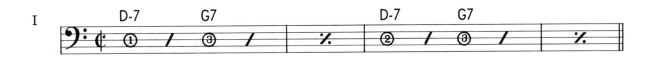

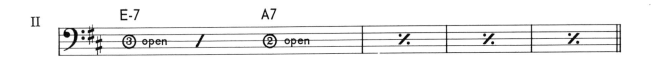

VI

D-7 G7 G-7 C7 C-7 F7

F-7 Bb7 Bb-7 Eb7 Eb-7 Ab7 Ab-7 Db7

Db-7 Gb7 F#-7 B7 B-7 E7 E-7 A7

A-7 D7 D-7 G7 G-7 C7 F

Minor Seventh (Major Sixth) Inversions

Notation-wise, the min 7th and major 6 chords are identical in their related places. For example, the C6 and the A-7 have the same notes. (CEGA). Naturally, the C6 should be understood from a 'C' root and the A-7 from the 'A' root. Some of the older orchestrations miscall these chords. (C6 instead of A-7). This, of course, is wrong and creates a minor third interval in the bass (lower) registers. The guitarist should be careful, therefore, *not to* make these substitutions.

Some of these inversion forms have already been diagramed in the "INVERSIONS OF THE ROOT POSITION MAJOR SIXTH CHORDS" (page 67). We take them up now as pure inversions of the upper structures of the sixth/minor seventh chords.

C6/A-7 TONIC NOTES (Not Relative Minor) CIRCLED.

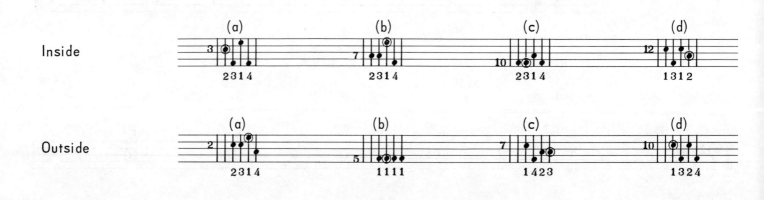

F6/D-7

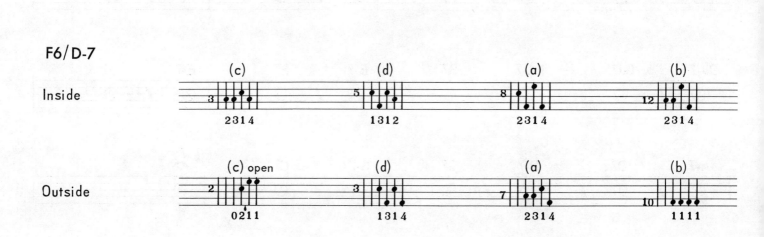

B♭6/G-7

Inside

Outside

E♭6/C-7

Inside

Outside

A♭6/F-7

Inside

Outside

D♭6/B♭-7

Inside

Outside

Gb6/Eb-7

Inside

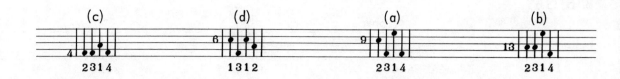

Outside

B6/G#-7

Inside

Outside

E6/C#-7

Inside

Outside

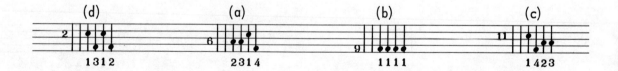

A6/F#-7

Inside

Outside

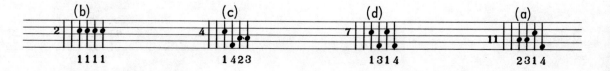

D6/B-7

Inside

D6/B-7

Outside

G6/E-7

Inside

G6/E-7

Outside

These 6th/min7 voicings would be referred to as 'open voicings' and, like the dominant seventh inversions, are voiced, as they are, by lowering the second tone from the top of the grouping by one octave:

This sequence, especially the rotation pattern of these forms, should be memorized.

Inside   Outside

	Inside					Outside			
C6 / A–7	(a)		(b)	(c)	(d)	⟶	(a)		(b)	(c)	(d)
F6 / D–7	(c)		(d)	(a)	(b)	⟶	(c)	open	(d)	(a)	(b)
B♭6 / G–7	(a)	open	(b)	(c)	(d)	⟶	(b)		(c)	(d)	(a)
E♭6 / C–7	(c)	open	(d)	(a)	(b)	⟶	(d)		(a)	(b)	(c)
A♭6 / F–7	(b)		(c)	(d)	(a)	⟶	(b)		(c)	(d)	(a)
D♭6 / B♭–7	(a)		(b)	(c)	(d)	⟶	(a)		(b)	(c)	(d)
G♭6 / E♭–7	(c)		(d)	(a)	(b)	⟶	(c)		(d)	(a)	(b)
B6 / G#–7	(a)		(b)	(c)	(d)	⟶	(a)	open	(b)	(c)	(d)
E6 / C#–7	(c)		(d)	(a)	(b)	⟶	(d)		(a)	(b)	(c)
A6 / F#–7	(b)		(c)	(d)	(a)	⟶	(b)		(c)	(d)	(a)
D6 / B–7	(d)		(a)	(b)	(c)	⟶	(d)	open	(a)	(b)	(c)
G6 / E–7	(b)	open	(c)	(d)	(a)	⟶	(b)	open	(c)	(d)	(a)

Alterations of the Minor Seventh Chord

The Minor Seventh Flat Five   I   ♭III   ♭V   ♭VII   Chord Symbol Example: C–7♭5

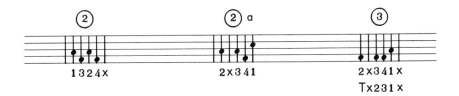

The minor triad is obvious in all three basic forms and expansion of the chordal and melodic possibilities is made simple by working with these triads.

Here is one method of determining the correct triad:

upper structure   (Given Chord)

(E♭ –)   C– 7♭5

Step 1 – Determine the relative tonic of C-7 (E♭)

Step 2 – The ♭5 of the C-7♭5 (G♭) would then make the (E♭) an (E♭ minor).

By this method, determine the min triad in the following chords:

A–7♭5(C–)   D–7♭5( )
C♯–7♭5( )   A♭–7♭5( )
B♭–7♭5( )   F–7♭5( )
E–7♭5( )   B–7♭5( )
G♭–7♭5( )   E♭–7♭5( )

The basic resolution of the min 7♭5 chord is to a dom7 a *fourth step* above.

Example:

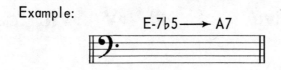

Find:

Example I

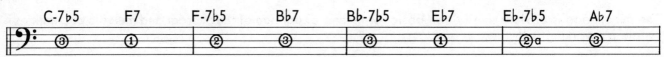

Example II

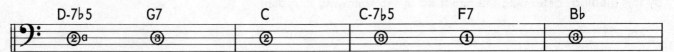

THE MAJOR SEVENTH CHORDS

I III V ♮VII

Chord Symbol Example: C Major 7 or C⑦

The major seventh chords (♮VII) have a different resolution than the dom or min 7th (♭VII). The maj 7th chords usually resolve to a (I maj 6.)

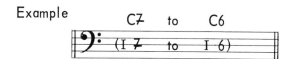

Example

C⑦ to C6

(I ⑦ to I 6)

The dom 7th and min 7th chords, as you recall, generally resolve to the IV above.

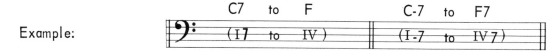

Example:

C7 to F   C-7 to F7

(I7 to IV)   (I-7 to IV7)

Basic Forms

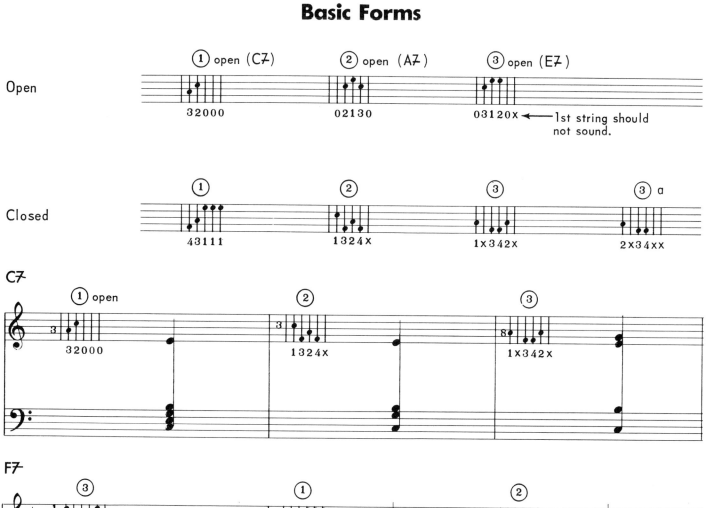

Open

① open (C⑦)   ② open (A⑦)   ③ open (E⑦)

32000   02130   03120x ← 1st string should not sound.

Closed

①   ②   ③   ③ a

43111   1324x   1x342x   2x34xx

C⑦

① open   ②   ③

32000   1324x   1x342x

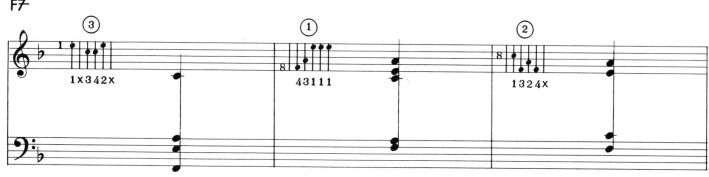

F⑦

③   ①   ②

1x342x   43111   1324x

112

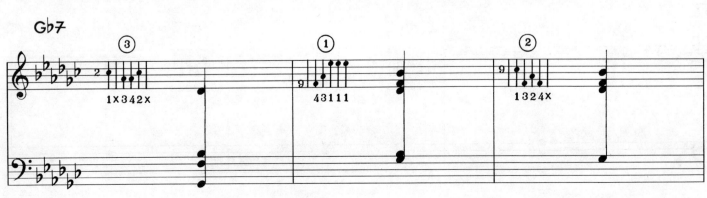

Memorize:

	col 1		col 2	col 3
C7	(1)	open	(2)	(3)
F7	(3)		(1)	(2)
B♭7	(2)		(3)	(1)
E♭7	(1)		(2)	(3)
A♭7	(3)		(1)	(2)
D♭7	(1)		(2)	(3)
G♭7	(3)		(1)	(2)
B7	(2)		(3)	(1)
E7	(3)	open	(1)	(2)
A7	(2)	open	(3)	(1)
D7	(1)		(2)	(3)
G7	(3)		(1)	(2)

You will notice the Minor Triad in the upper structure of the Major Seventh chords. These Triads can be inverted for expanded harmonized patterns or arpeggiated to form the beginning for melodic possibilities.

Major Seventh to Major Sixth Resolutions
Root Positions for Accompaniment and Rhythm

The major seventh to major sixth resolution is one of the most frequently used harmonic patterns. It is, therefore, advantageous to be able to play these patterns with ease and a minimum of physical effort.

The examples below should help the player develop skill in changing from the maj 7th to the maj 6th chords.

Example I

You will observe that the 3rd and 4th fingers are common to both chord forms. It will help, to concentrate on keeping these two fingers in place, therefore, changing only the 1st and 2nd fingers.
This exercise should be practiced until there is no excess effort needed to play this progression.

Example II

This is a very simple fingering pattern, as it only requires lifting the 3rd finger and noting the 1st finger down;

hence the reason behind the form ③a7̸ and the ③a6th.

Examples III+IV

These are combinations of two of the most commonly used progressions, the maj 7th to 6th and the min 7th to dom 7th.

(III)

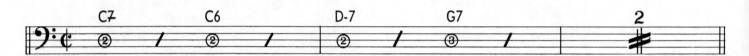

(IV)

*Try to figure out similar patterns in various keys.

Alterations of the Major Seventh Chords

I III +V ♮VII

Chord Symbol Example: C7̷(+5)

BASIC FORMS

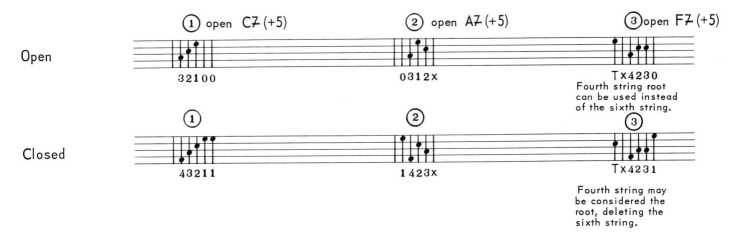

Open

① open C7̷ (+5)   32100

② open A7̷ (+5)   0312x

③ open F7̷ (+5)   Tx4230
Fourth string root
can be used instead
of the sixth string.

Closed

①   43211

②   1423x

③   Tx4231
Fourth string may
be considered the
root, deleting the
sixth string.

The maj 7(+5) chord is usually used as a passing chord when the same maj 7th chord remains in use for an extended period.

Example

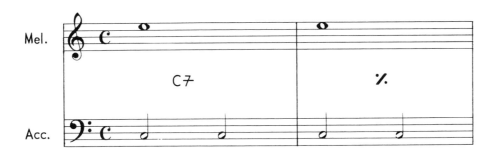

Mel.

C7̷   %.

Acc.

In a situation such as this, by raising the Vth of the the chord ½ step each two beats, you can get a very pleasant harmonic pattern. (See Example I, page 118)

Note the interesting pattern resulting from the insertion of the C7(+5) chord.

Example I

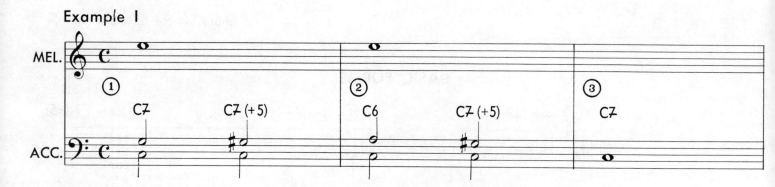

In this example, the chord in bar ③ would most likely be a Cmaj or Cmaj 7

If, however, the chord in Bar ③ were an F chord, the pattern would most likely be:

Example II

The following pattern has been used frequently in many songs and arrangements.

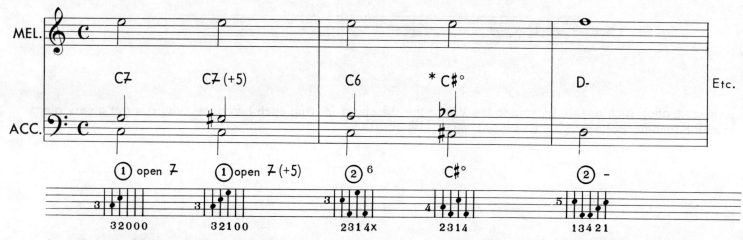

Attention should be called to the major triad in the upper structure of the maj7(+5). This triad can serve as a simple component to work to expand your harmonic and melodic ideas.

* C♯ DIMINISHED CHORD.

THE MINOR NATURAL SEVEN CHORDS

I ♭III V ♮VII   Chord Symbol Example: C–(♮7) or C–7̵

(This chord is also referred to as the Minor-Major Seventh Chord.)

Having the ♮VII above the minor triad, the min (♮7) can resolve to a min 6th.

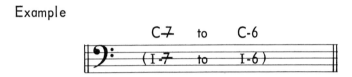

The min 7̵. chord is also used as a passing chord to accommodate a melody or secondary melody. When used for this purpose, the progression will usually be:

Example

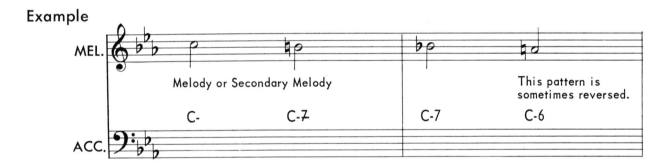

BASIC FORMS

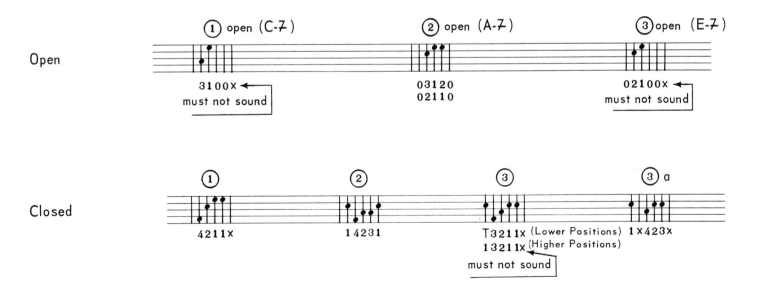

*(Form ③ a may be preferred over Form ③ .

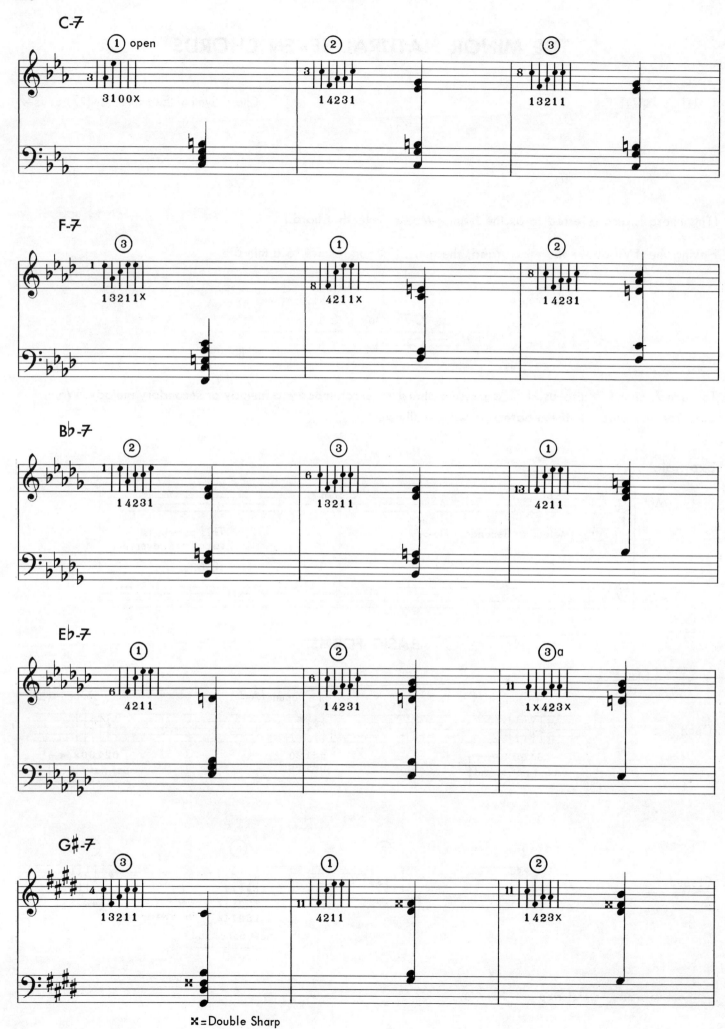

x = Double Sharp

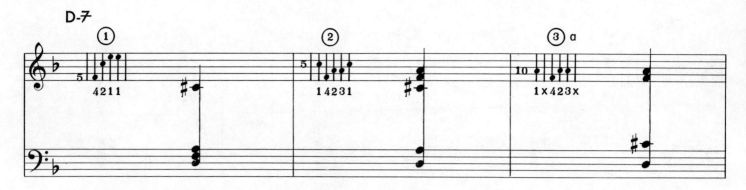

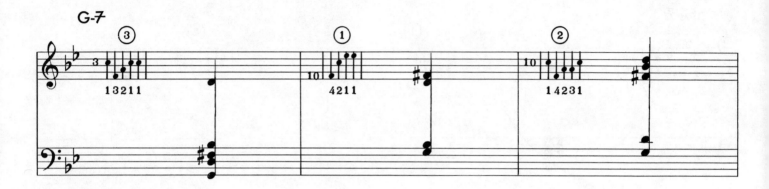

MEMORIZE:

C-7	① open	②	③
F-7	③	①	②
Bb-7	②	③	①
Eb-7	①	②	③
G#-7	③	①	②
C#-7	①	②	③
F#-7	③	①	②
B-7	②	③	①
E-7	③ open	①	②
A-7	② open	③	①
D-7	①	②	③
G-7	③	①	②

The upper structure of the min 7 is an augmented chord. Complete study of the augmented chord will be in
VOLUME II.

Resolution Exercises for the Minor Natural Seven to Minor Sixth

Example I

(Note common fingers to both chord forms.)

Example II

Exercises with the Minor Natural Seven Used As a Passing Chord

Example I

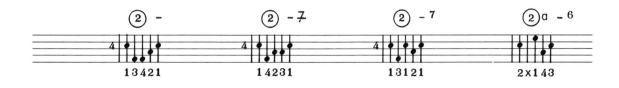

Example II

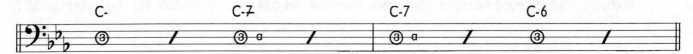

Exercises Combining Two Basic Resolutions

Minor 7 to Minor 6 and Minor 7♭5 to Dominant 7th.

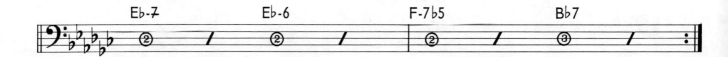

*(Note common fingerings)

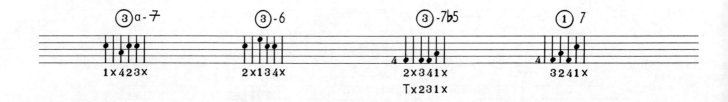

PART TWO

In thinking of a Student-Teacher relationship, one point overrides all the rest. The true mark of a good teacher is the ability and integrity to get the students to a level, so that the students can start to help themselves. This can only be possible by giving the student complete and clearly understood fundamentals to work from. If this is not done, there is no way that the student can ever be anything but a student. Individualism (style) cannot be taught and has to be developed by the individual.

It is not practical or possible to write actual songs to which the chords and chord patterns in this book will fit. The important thing to keep in mind is the fact that melodies are most often inspired by chord patterns. This point is certainly proven by musicians who can improvise lovely melodies, spontaneously, to fit given harmonic patterns.

J.S.

INTRODUCTION TO PART TWO

The knowledge, understanding and ability to reduce extended and intricate harmonic structures (chords) to a simple component, makes it immediately possible for the player to create melodic or chordal melodies or counter melodies. All extended, tonal, harmonic structures with the exception of the SIX/NINE and the MINOR SIX/NINE, can be reduced to a simple component. These components will generally appear in the upper structures of chords and usually be unrelated to the root name of the chord. As an example (mentioned in Part I, pg. 42) the E major triad in the upper structure of a G 13♭9,

is not related to the G root, but it serves as a simple and effective component to work with to create chordal or melodic passages to fit the texture and sound of this chord. We will refer to these components as UPPER STRUCTURE COMPONENTS. Basically there are FOUR UPPER STRUCTURE COMPONENTS. THESE COMPONENTS ARE:

      1. THE MAJOR TRIAD
      2. THE MINOR TRIAD
      3. THE MAJOR THIRD INTERVAL (augmented)
      4. THE MINOR THIRD INTERVAL (diminished)

The first two components (THE MAJOR AND MINOR TRIADS) were studied in Part I and the other two (THE MAJOR THIRD AND MINOR THIRD INTERVALS) will be studied in this part.

The AUGMENTED and the DIMINISHED SEVENTH chords are the only chords structured with *EQUALLY SPACED* intervals and these chords and their related scales and arpeggios must be thoroughly familiar to the musician so that the extended harmonies that include these components may be most simply and effectively utilized.

The Augmented Chord ✓

The augmented chord is structured with EQUALLY SPACED *MAJOR THIRD INTERVALS.*

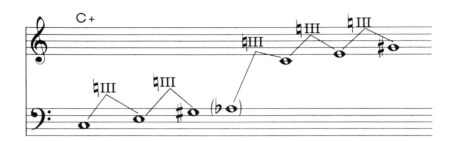

As this example shows, there are two WHOLE STEPS (ONE MAJOR THIRD INTERVAL) between each of the notes of this chord:

        (a) C to E
        (b) E to G♯
        (c) A♭ (G♯) to C   and etc.

Because of the equally spaced intervals that structure the augmented and diminished chords, these chords automatically invert *perfectly* when moved up or down to their respective interval.

As an example, the C+, E+, and G♯+ chords will have the same notes. Like the other chords, the augmented and diminished chords will be named from their root positions. The E+ and G♯+ **WOULD NOT** be considered as inversions of the C+ chord.

The augmented chord is basically a resolving chord with the exception of being used to accommodate a passing tone such as the example shown in Part I (pg. **118**). The augmented chord will usually PROGRESS to a *FOURTH* or a *HALF STEP* ABOVE.

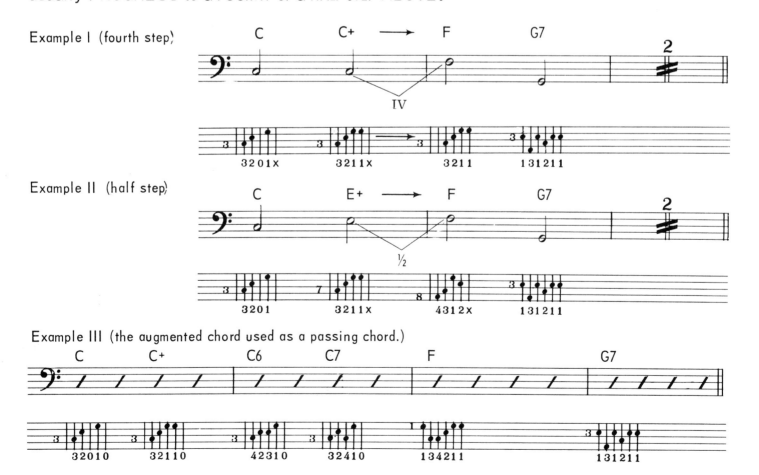

The Basic Form Augmented Chords ✓

(MAJOR THIRD INTERVALS)　　　Chord symbol Example: C aug. or C+

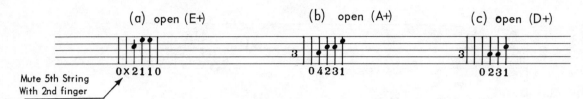

These forms would be used mostly for rhythm or accompaniment in the lower positions.

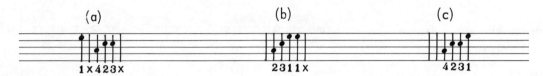

Forms (a) and (b) would be used primarily as rhythm or accompaniment chord forms and named from the notes on the sixth or fifth strings. Form (c) would be used most frequently as a melodic chord because of it being pitched higher, and could be identified by any note of the chord form, however, note that I use the term *IDENTIFIED, NOT NAMED.*

Progressions Using the Augmented Chords ✓

(Repeat all exercises as needed for memorization)

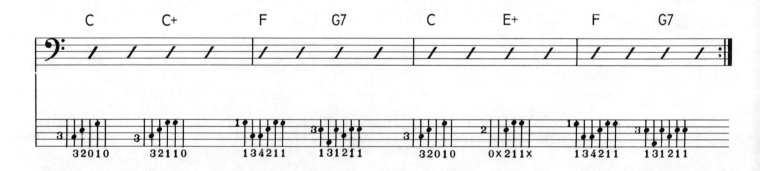

NOTE:　　When a note is not indicated in the upper part of a chord diagram, the string should not sound even though it is not designated as such by an (x).

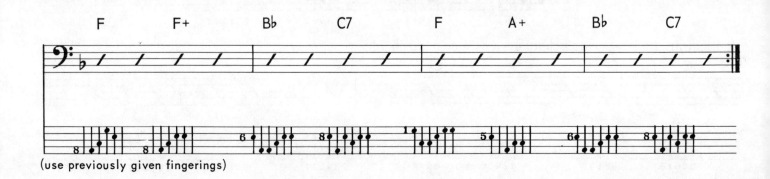

(use previously given fingerings)

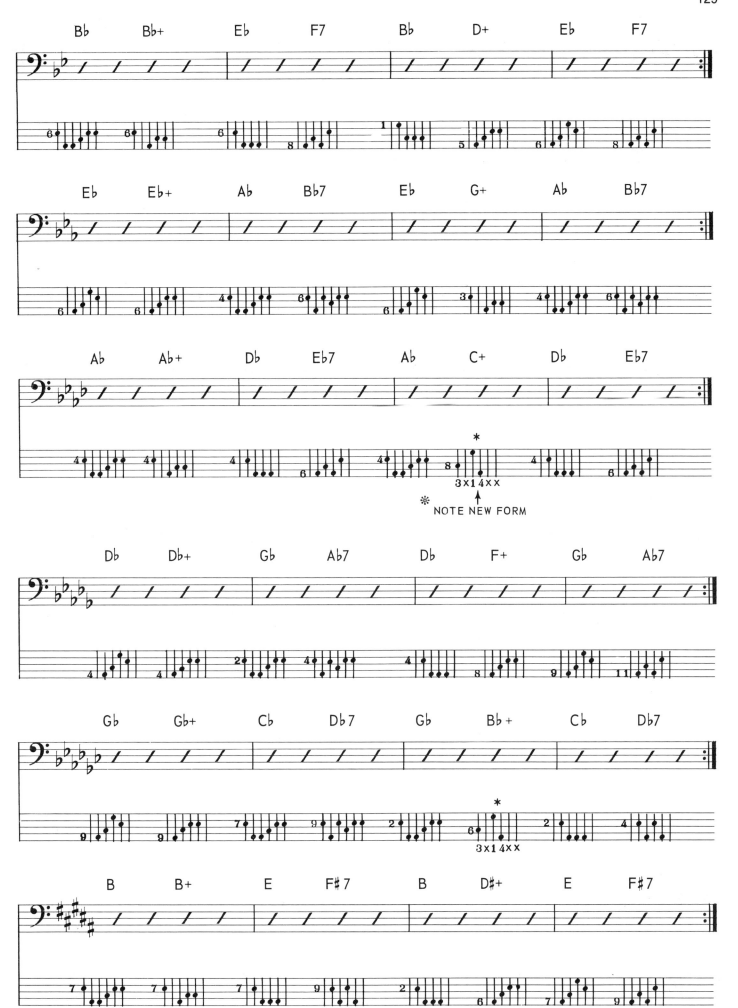

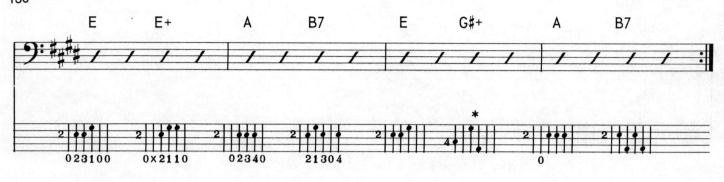

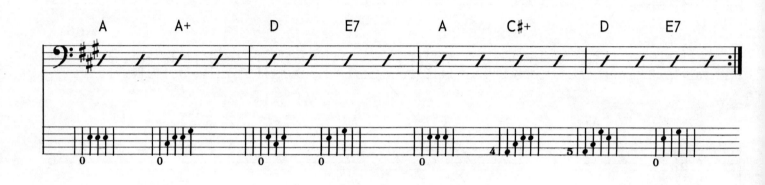

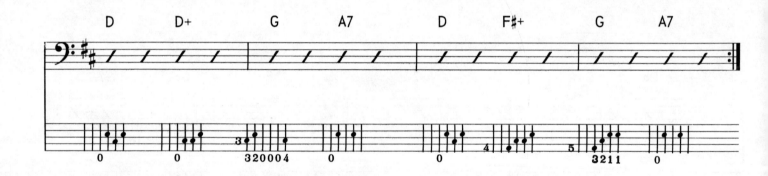

Student should work out similar exercises in the keys of E, A, and D using all closed forms instead of the open forms given.

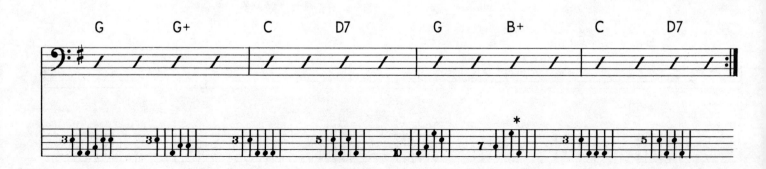

Augmented Arpeggio Studies

These are two octave, basic form arpeggio studies with starting notes on the sixth and fifth strings. Like the scale and arpeggio exercises in Part I, these arpeggios should be played as legato as possible with alternating picking maintained throughout. The arpeggio forms and the position-shift spacing should be memorized as soon as possible so that the actual playing/practice of the arpeggios can be more precise and musical.

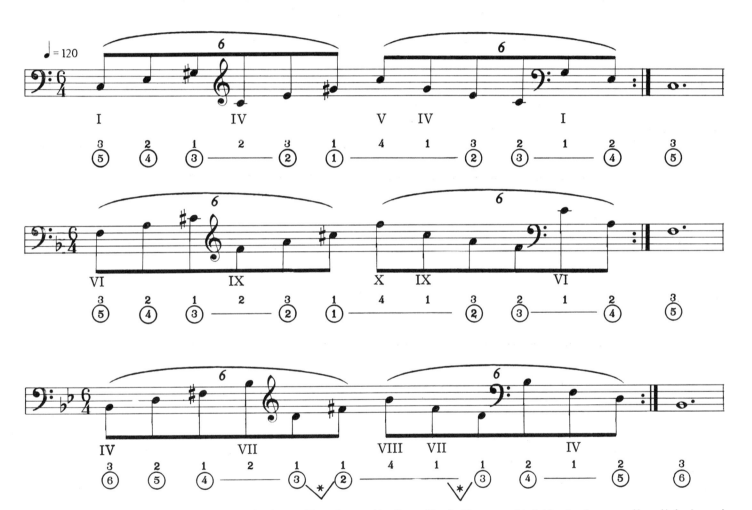

NOTE: Try to roll the first finger slightly between the third and second strings to avoid a bar. The bar would break the continuity (evenness) of the arpeggio. This to apply to all arpeggios starting on the sixth string.

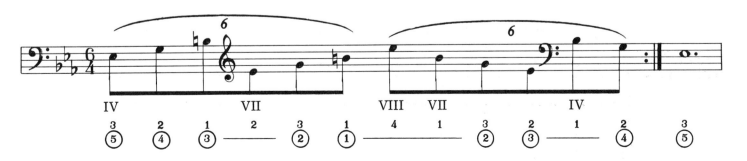

132

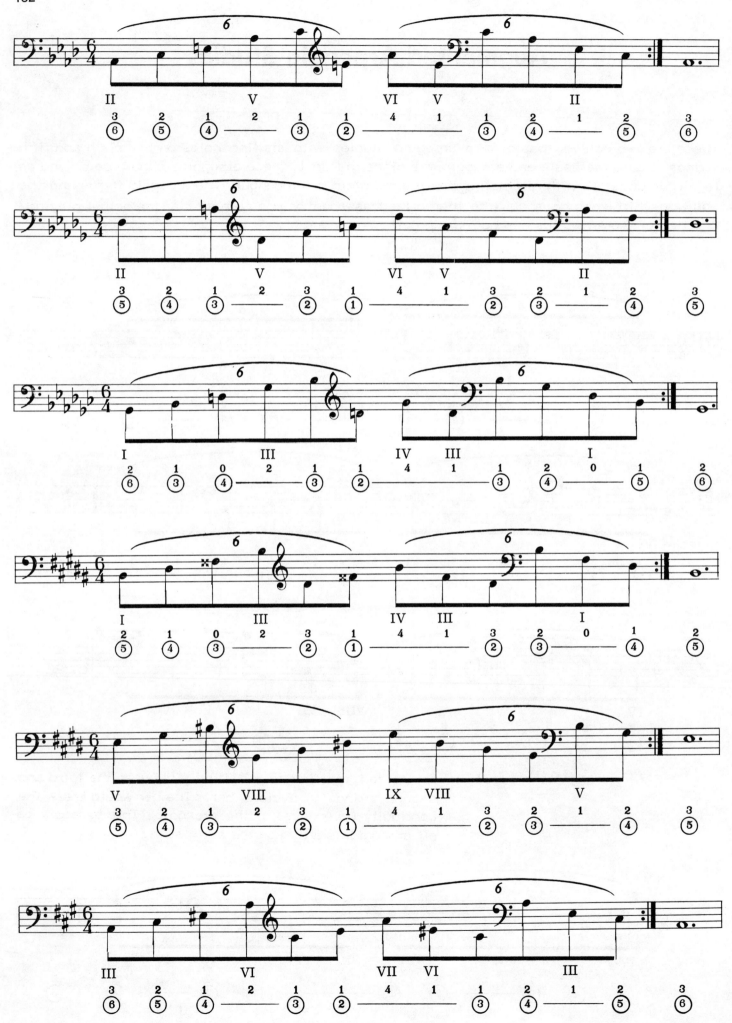

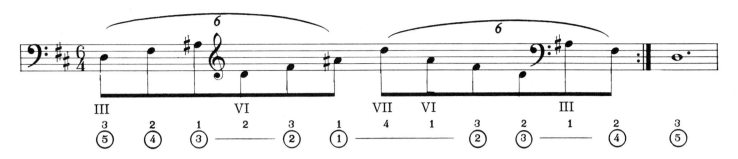

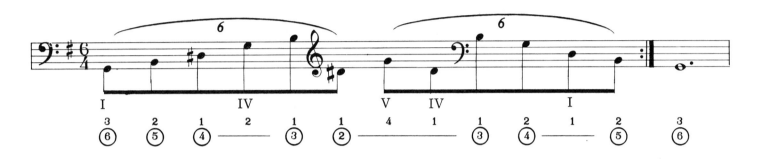

Some of the arpeggio studies can be played with the same pitch but starting on a different string in the same key. Others can be played an octave higher in the same key. Using fingerings already given, work out the following arpeggios:

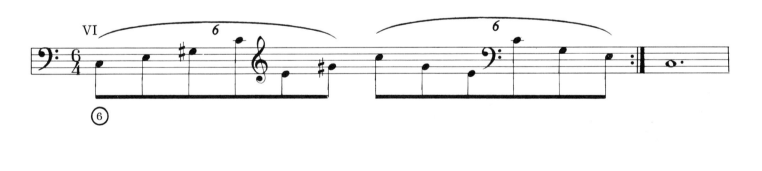

134

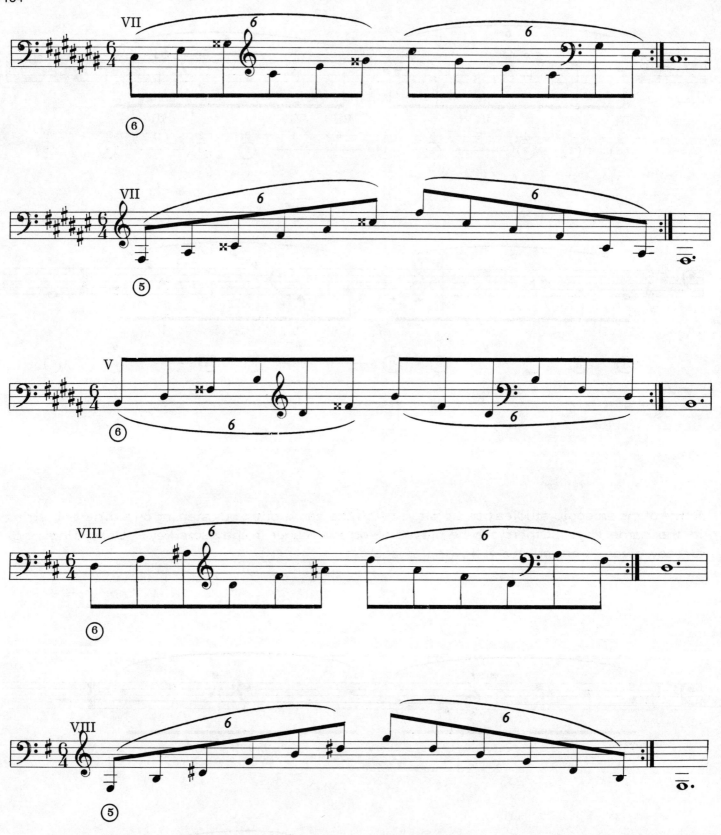

The different fingering and position possibilities, plus extended or deleted ranges for the Aug. arpeggios, makes it impractical to try to write them all. It is important, however, to keep in mind that: *Each one of these arpeggios is applicable to three augmented chords.*

The three chords can be identified by the *first three notes of each arpeggio.* For example, the C+ arpeggio is also opplicable to the E+ and the G♯+ chords.

List the related augmented chords to the following:

G+	_____	_____	Db+	_____	_____
D+	_____	_____	Ab+	_____	_____
A+	_____	_____	Eb+	_____	_____
E+	_____	_____	Bb+	_____	_____
B+	_____	_____	F+	_____	_____
Gb+	_____	_____	C+	_____	_____

The Augmented Scales

The augmented scale is commonly referred to as the WHOLE TONE SCALE, the whole step being a perfect division of the major third interval. The whole tone scale is directly related to the augmented chord and the augmented arpeggio.

The fingerings worked out for these scales form two distinctly different patterns. Concentration on the first two scales until these patterns are familiar, will make it easy to continue through the cycle. These patterns should facilitate the performance of the scales at various speeds.

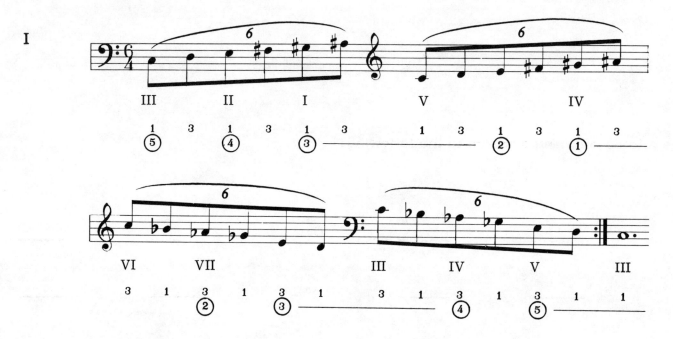

NOTE: Positions are numbered by first finger but with a major third interval spread on each string. (Whole step between 1st and 2nd, 2nd and 4th fingers.) *THIS APPLIES TO THE SCALES THAT START ON THE SIXTH STRING ONLY.*

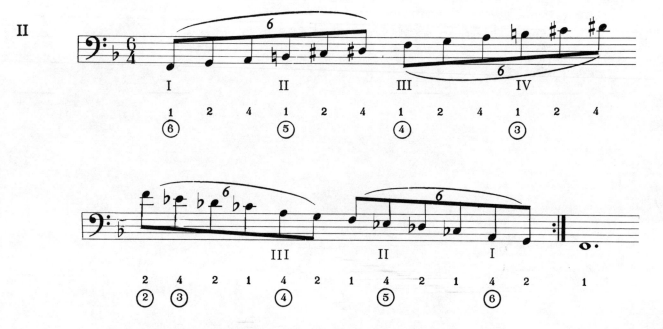

NOTE: Encompassing the major third interval on one string takes us outside the normal *four fret/four finger* left hand position. This wide finger spread will be easier accomplished if the thumb is kept in back of the neck and in back of the second finger. The thumb should be moved respectively with each position shift.

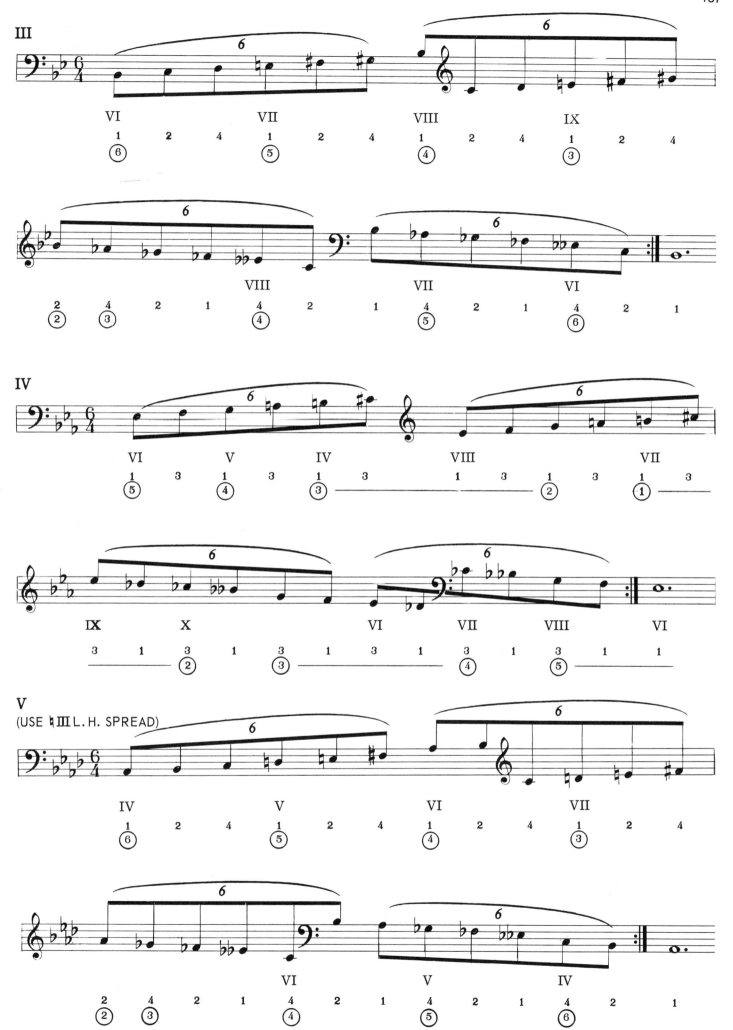

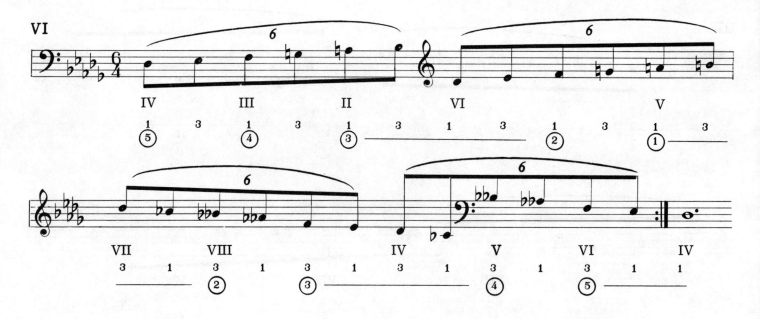

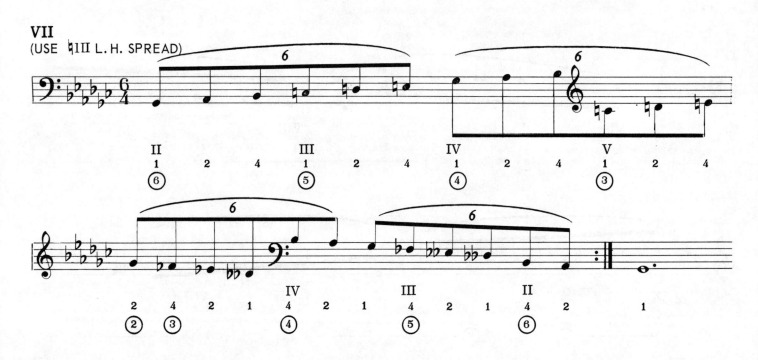

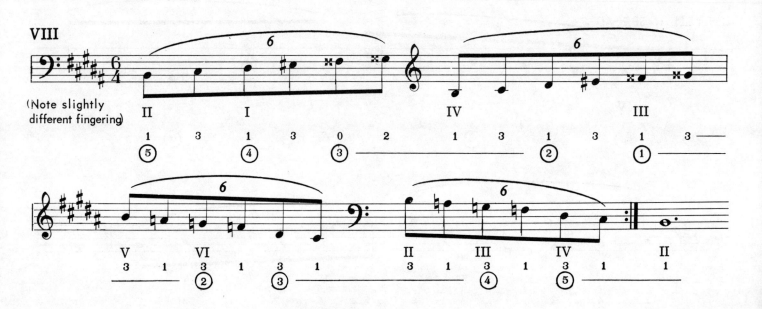

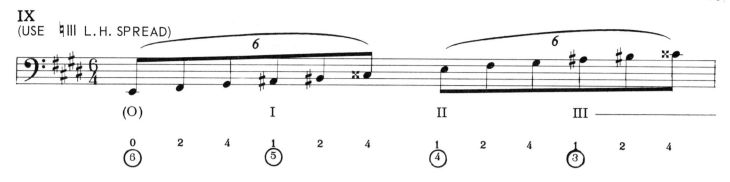

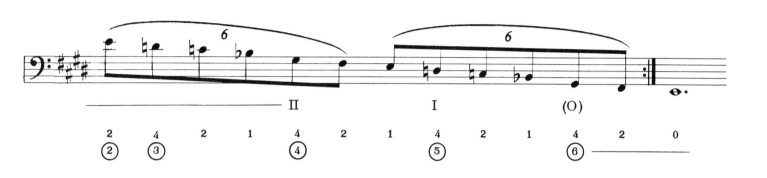

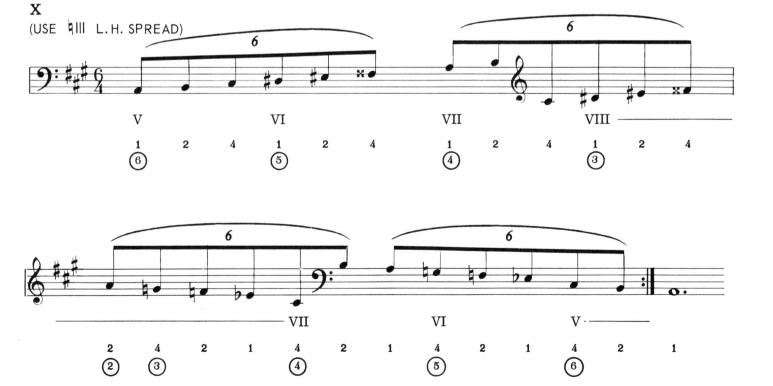

XI

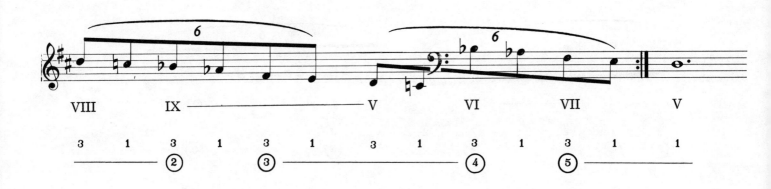

XII

(USE ♮III L.H. SPREAD)

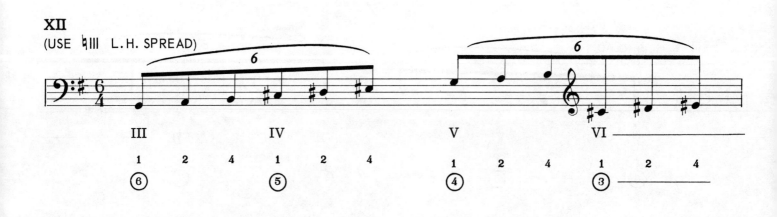

Application of the Augmented Arpeggios and Scales

The augmented chord, augmented arpeggio and scale, being structured from the MAJOR THIRD INTERVAL, is one of the UPPER STRUCTURE COMPONENTS. The augmented chords, arpeggios and scales can be used with chord structures other than augmented chord progressions themselves.

The AUGMENTED CHORD is aligned tonally, with the 7b5 CHORD (See Part I, pg. 96). To establish this fact, take as example the Gb7b5 chord and the C+ chord.

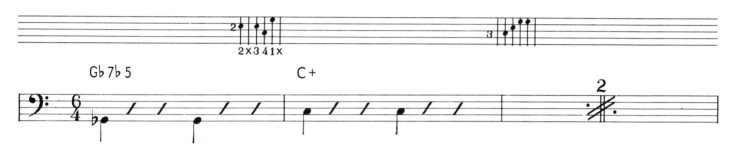

In playing and alternating the Gb7b5 with the C+ you can hear a very definite similarity of chord type between the two chords. This being a fact would also establish the fact that the C+ *ARPEGGIOS AND SCALES COULD BE USED RELATIVE TO THE Gb7b5.*

For an example, play:

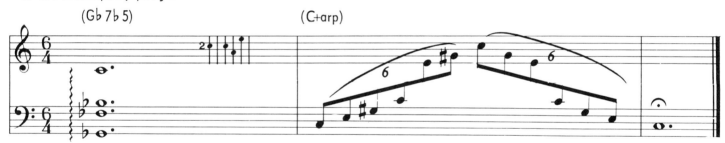

For an example using the augmented (whole tone) scale, play:

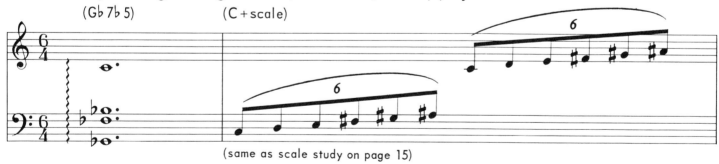

(same as scale study on page 15)

The creation of a melodic line to fit the Gb7b5 was made possible and simple by the application of the augmented arpeggio and scale. These examples only establish the fact that the upper structure components, when correctly related to the given chord, are theoretically sound. The countless melodic ideas, possible through experimentation, are limited only by the individual. Try working out the augmented arpeggios and scales for the following 7♭5 chords: (AVOID, IF POSSIBLE, STARTING BELOW THE PITCH OF THE ROOT NOTE. USE SUGGESTED START-ING NOTES)

C7♭5   (start from I)

F7♭5   (start from I)

B♭7♭5   (start from ♭V)

E♭7♭5   (start from I)

A♭7♭5   (start from ♭V)

D♭7♭5   (start from I)

B7♭5   (start from I)

E7♭5   (start from I)

A7♭5   (start from ♭V)

D7♭5   (start from I)

G7♭5   (start from ♭V)

Augmented arpeggios and scales can be further utilized with the Augmented Eleventh Chord.

The Diminished Seventh Chord

The diminished seventh chord is structured with equally spaced MINOR THIRD INTERVALS.

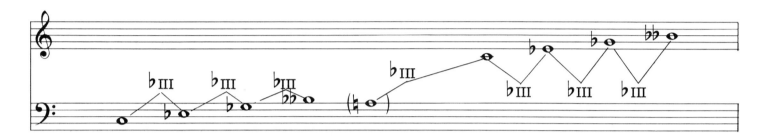

There always seems to be an element of confusion in the analyzation of the diminished seventh chord and the reason for naming the chord as such, when in reality, every note above the root of a dominant seventh chord has been lowered (diminished). For example, take the C7 and C dim. 7 chords:

By calling the double flat seventh note of a diminished seventh chord by different name, and relating it to the root accordingly, we find that a diminished seventh chord could be identified as a MINOR SIX FLAT FIVE CHORD.

The main reason for not calling a (dim 7) chord a (min 6♭5) is the fact that any chord containing a ♭V will usually resolve to a lower chord or a chord a fourth step above. The diminished seventh can resolve a half step lower as well as a half step higher.

We will refer to the two types of resolutions of the diminished seventh chord as MODES:

1. ASCENDING MODE

2. DESCENDING MODE

Example I (ascending mode)

Example II (descending mode)

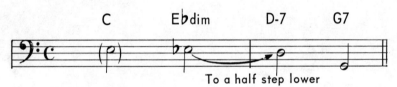

Supplements to the above progressions will be studied subsequently.

Basic Form Diminished Seventh Chords

Example of chord symbol: (C dim) or (C°)

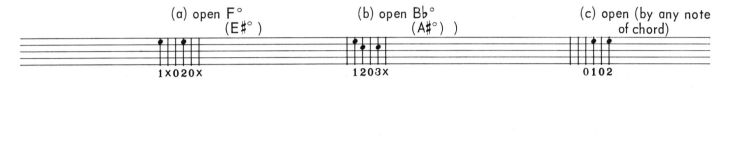

(a) open F°
(E♯°)

(b) open B♭°
(A♯°)

(c) open (by any note of chord)

1 X 0 2 0 X   1 2 0 3 X   0 1 0 2

(a)   (b)   (b) alt   (c)

2 X 1 3 1 X   2 3 1 4 X   2 X 1 4 1   1 3 2 4

Forms (a) and (b) would be used most frequently as rhythm or accompaniment chord forms and named from the root notes on the sixth or fifth strings. Form (c) would be used more frequently as a melodic chord because of being pitched higher and could be identified by any note of the chord form. Note once again that I use the word   *IDENTIFIED, NOT NAMED.*

Progressions Using the Diminished Seventh Chords

When the diminished chord is used in a descending mode, the preceeding major or major sixth chord may be inverted to the first inversion (III in the bass) to further add to the continuity of the descending bass line.

(Review Part I for SIXTH and inverted SIXTH chords.)

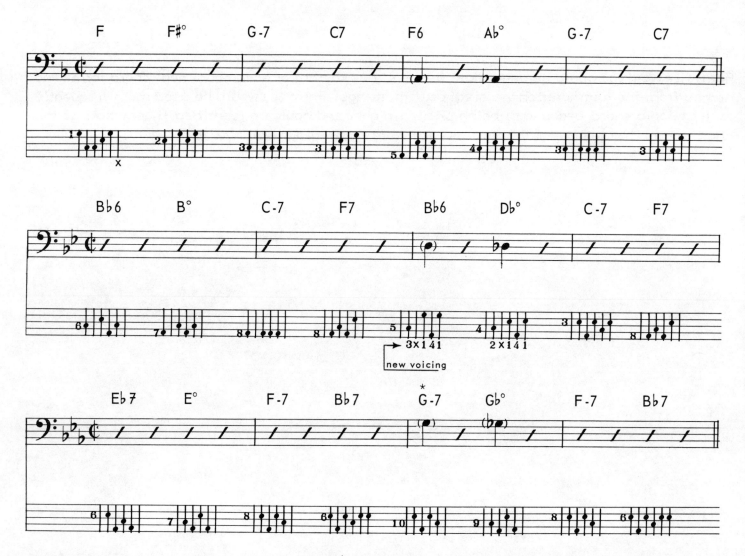

* G-7 being substituted for the inverted Eb maj 9 chord. The inverted Eb maj 9 is an extension of the inverted Eb 7 chord. Deletion of notes in some of the chord forms is done so that the top notes of the forms create a melodic line.

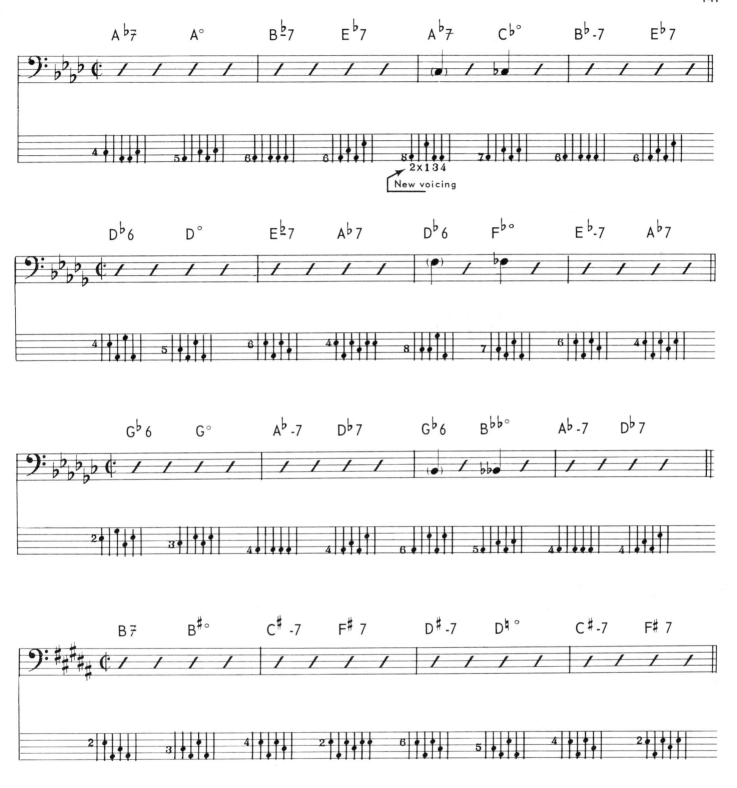

The next three exercises use the diminished chord with some open string chord forms.

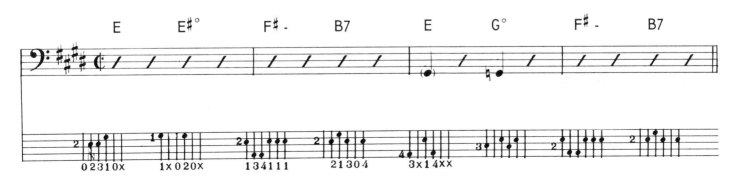

148

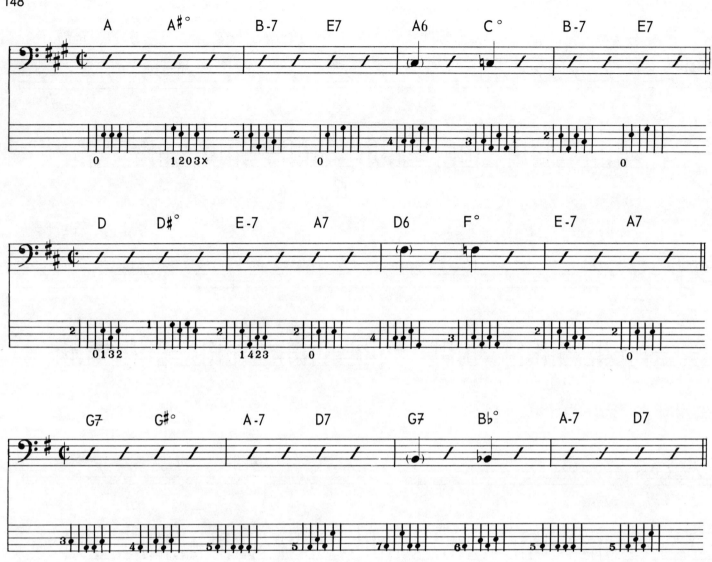

In all the preceeding exercises the diminished chord has resolved to a minor seventh chord. There are situations, due to thé melody note, that makes it mandatory to resolve directly to the dominant seventh. Here is an example of such a melody:

As you can see, the Eb° is not a half step away from G7. In a situation like this, the G7 would be inverted to it's second inversion (V or D in the bass). This would then give us the half step resolution of Eb, to D·

Example

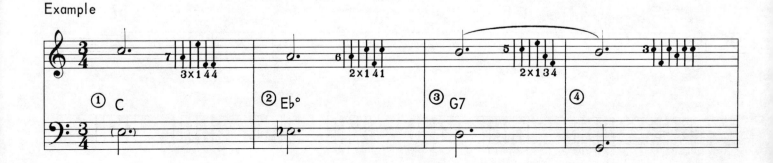

The D bass in bar ③ leading to the G bass in bar ④ gives us a resolution even though the chord (G7) remains the same. Below, is a similar situation with the diminished being used in an ascending mode.

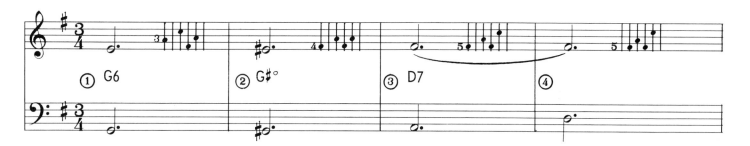

There are some songs that use the diminished in a non-resolving way. This is usually done to accommodate a half step melodic phrase with the root note remaining the same.

Example

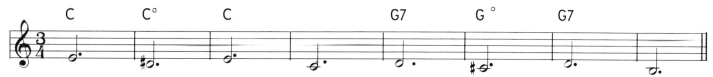

In a situation such as this; the chords would be played as shown.

Because of older concepts, diminished chords are quite frequently misnamed (wrong root). Here are a couple of examples of misnaming the diminished chord by wrongly naming the chord by any note of the structure.

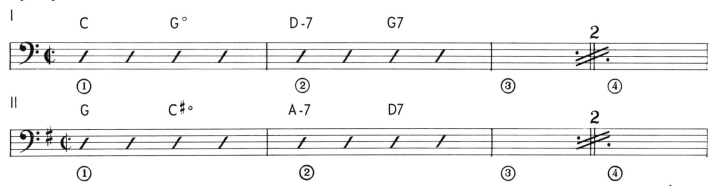

The names of the diminished chords can be corrected by picking out the note of the diminished chord that is a half step away from the resolving chord or the bass note should the chord be inverted (as shown in the preceeding examples).

In example I, the 'G' root is not a half step interval from the 'D' root so we would want to find which note of a G° chord is. First, assertain the notes of a G° chord:

The only note in a G° chord that is a half step interval from D is C#, therefore, the diminished chord should be called C#°.

In example II in determining the notes in the C#° chord:

we find that the only note a half step away from the 'A' root in bar ② is Bb therefore, the C#° should have been named a Bb° chord.

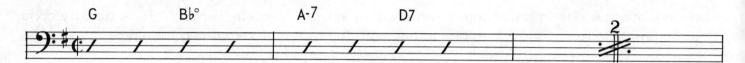

Correct the names of the diminished chords in the following examples:

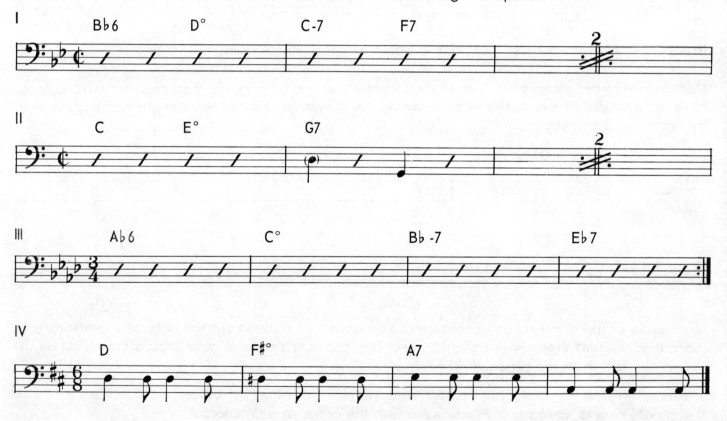

In this example, bar ② has the correct notes in the bass (D#), therefore the diminished should be D#° in bar 2. In most instances, especially working with sheet music, the correct diminished chord name can be immediately assertained by looking at the *bass note* in the bass clef.

Chord symbols are only valid and acceptable musically when they are *correctly named and understood.* Emphasis is again placed on the importance of co-relating the chord name with the bass note. A chord symbol, correctly stated, is not only valid for the guitar but for other instruments as well or in fact, the entire orchestra.

Diminished Arpeggio Studies

These two octave diminished arpeggio studies are, basically, two closely related forms, one form starting from the fifth string and the other from the sixth string. Familiarization of the fingering patterns and position shifts of forms 1 and 2, initially, will make it easy to play them throughout all keys.

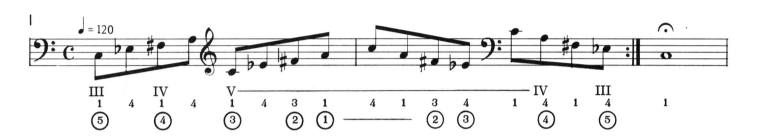

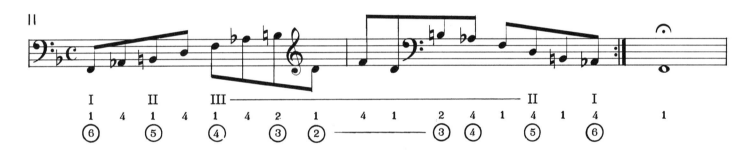

* similar fingering patterns and position shifts can be noted between these two basic forms.

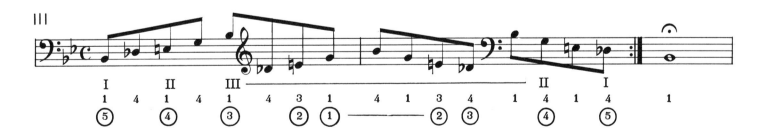

152

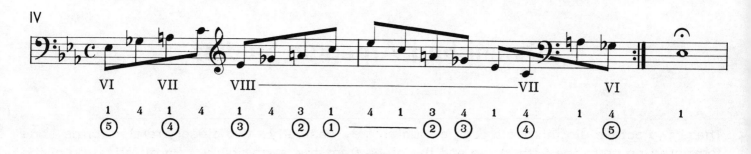

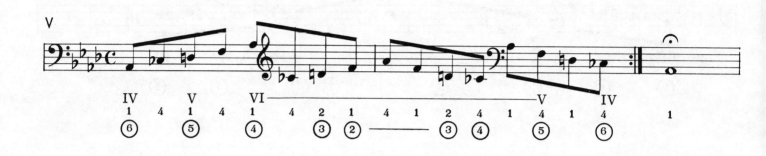

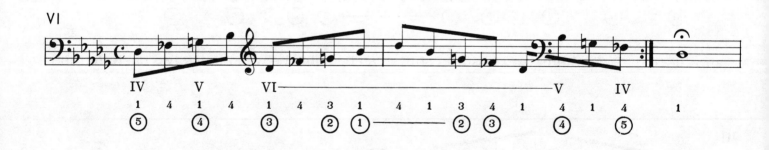

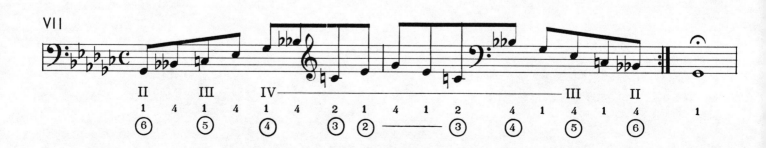

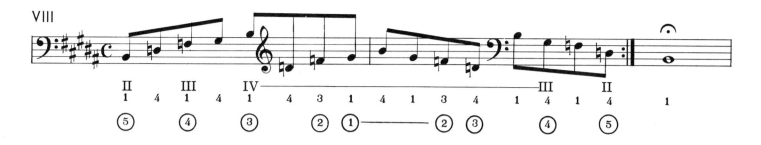

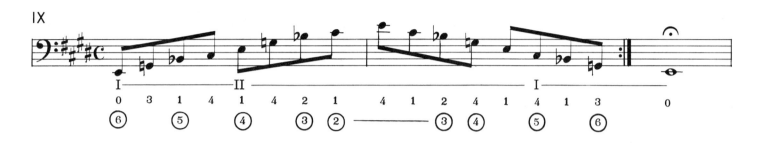

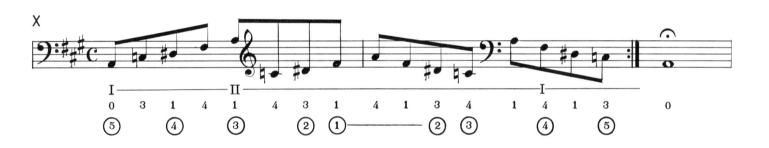

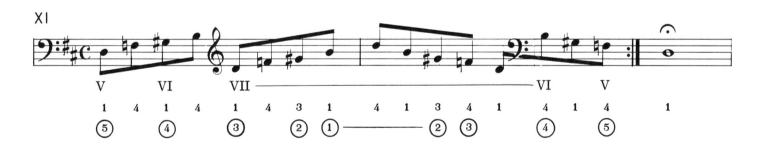

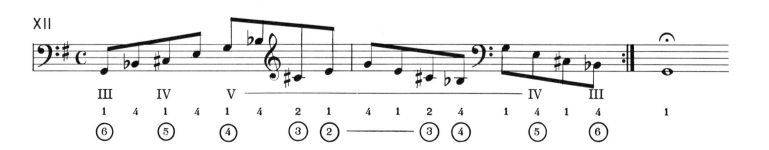

154

From fingerings used in the preceeding exercises,
work out the following supplemental arpeggios :

The Diminished Scale Studies

The diminished scale is also known as the EIGHT TONE SCALE and the WHOLE TONE-HALF TONE SCALE. Other than a chromatic division, the minor third interval can only be divided by a whole step and a half step. The diminished scale can be written and used two different ways.

Seg. I
By starting the scale sequence with a whole step:

This sequence would relate the diminished scale directly to the diminished chord. In simple terms, the scale sequence is created by preceeding each note of the diminished arpeggio with a half step.

Seg. II
By starting the scale sequence with a half step:

This sequence would relate the diminished scale to, and make it easy to create a melodic line for the following chords:

1. 7b9   2. 7(+9)   3. 7b9(+11)   4. 7#9(+11)

(These relationships will be established in subsequent sections of this text)

Because of the multiple use possibilities, these diminished scale studies will be on the second (II) sequence.

The diminished scale would be an extremely difficult scale to play without a simple fingering pattern (form). These scales are fingered from two basic forms (starting from the *fifth string* and starting from the *sixth string* and familiarization of forms 1 and 3 will make it easy to play the diminished scale in all keys simply by finding their locations on the fingerboard.

156

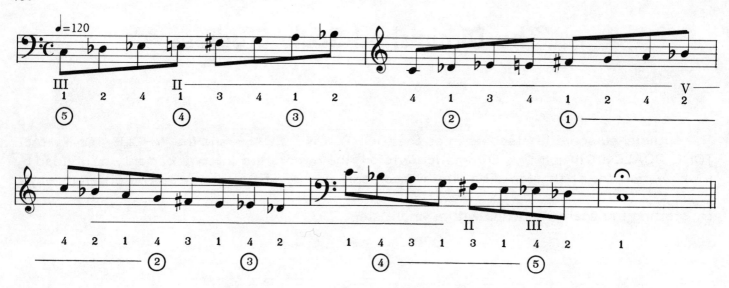

(By descending with a different pattern, this scale form is made more playable.)

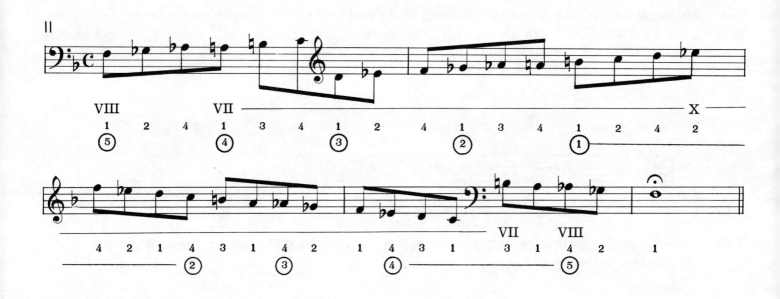

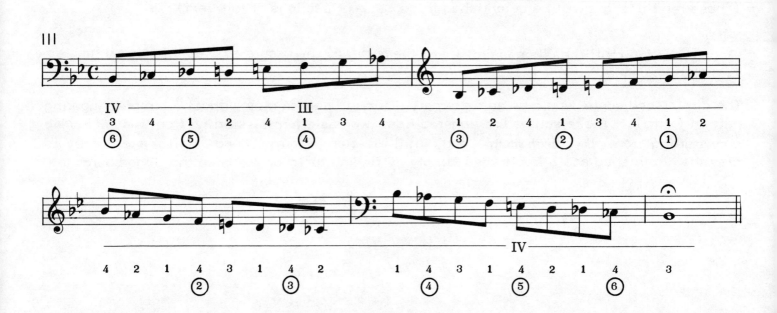

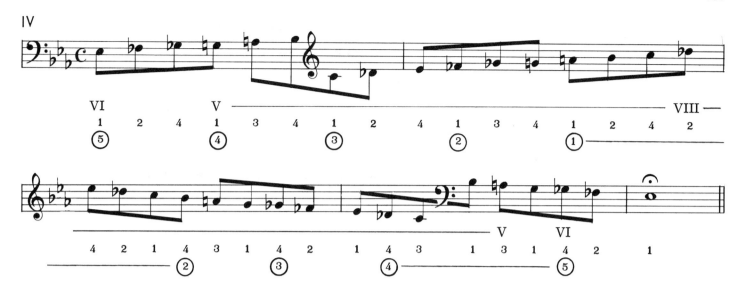

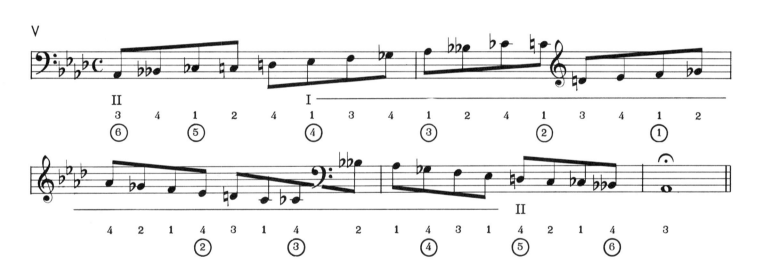

(Also learn this scale study starting on the sixth string)

VII

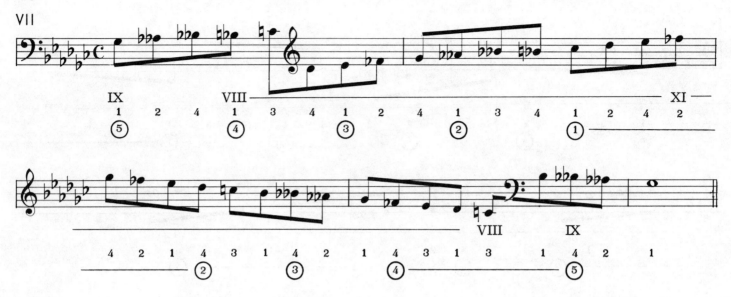

VIII

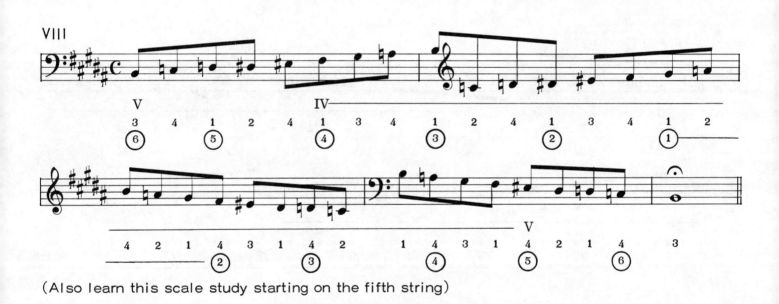

(Also learn this scale study starting on the fifth string)

IX

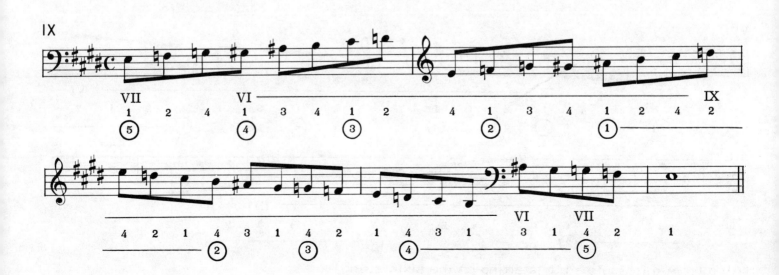

X

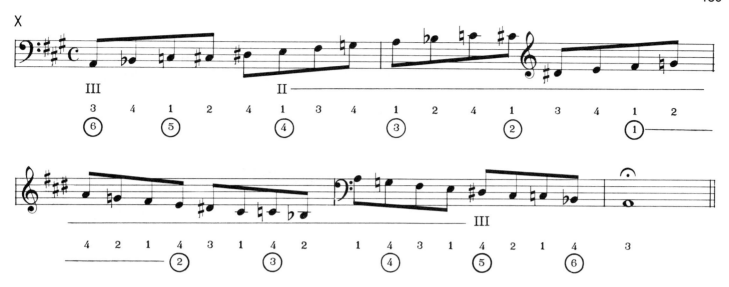

XI

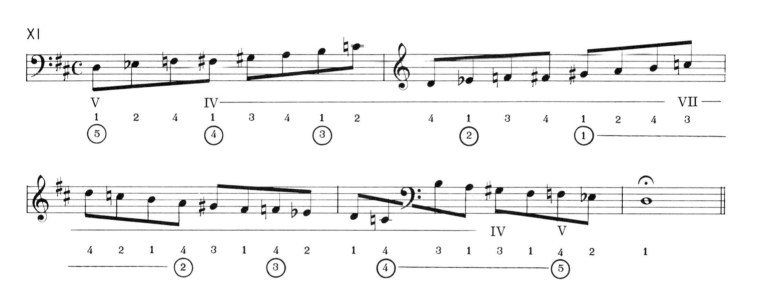

XII

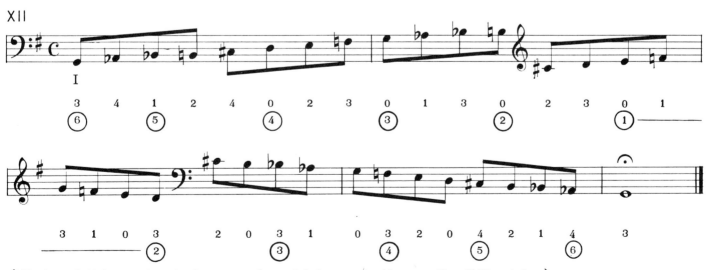

(Work out this scale study one octave higher, starting on the fifth string)

Many variations and patterns can be worked out using the diminished scale. This next example is an extended diminished scale using a triplet rhythm.　 It is interesting to note the fingering pattern on the descending segment of this scale.

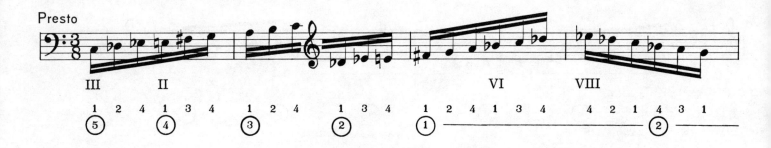

(Practice this study chromatically up as high as practical)

The Half Diminished Chord

The half diminished chord is structured and fingered the same and from the same root note as the minor seventh flat five but is named differently because it resolves differently. The half diminished was probably so named because of it's closeness in structure to a full diminished chord and the fact that it most frequently resolves to a full diminished.

One way to avoid confusion of the half diminished and the minor seventh flat five chord is to remember that the minor seventh flat five ALWAYS resolves to the IV 7 as shown in the examples below:

When the resolution is other than a fourth step,
the chord should be called a half diminished.

Here are some examples of the half diminished chord being used in various harmonic phrases:

Example I
Resolving to a full diminished chord

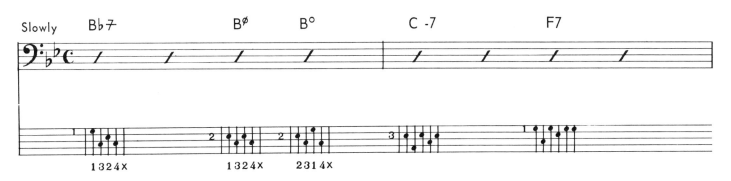

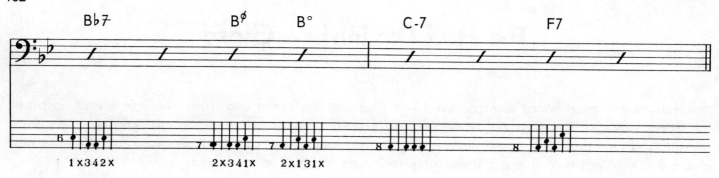

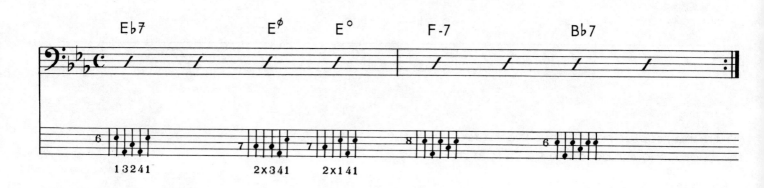

Example II
To accommodate a half step melodic line.

The Chromatic Scale Studies

All melodies are made with scales, arpeggios and combinations of the two. The knowledge and proficiency in playing of various types of scales and arpeggios should make it possible for the player to develop a prolific technique for melodic playing. Self-criticism for tonal quality and control of tempi combined with the above requisites should remove all limitations in melodic performance.

The chromatic scale studies are fingered and positioned from *two* basic forms (starting from the fifth and sixth strings) to make them playable and certain at various speeds. Study fingering patterns in exercises #I and #III before continuing through the cycle.

Note position change on fourth finger at the top of the scale sequence and on the first finger at the bottom. After recommended speed of the scales is attained, foot should be tapped **one beat to the bar**.

164

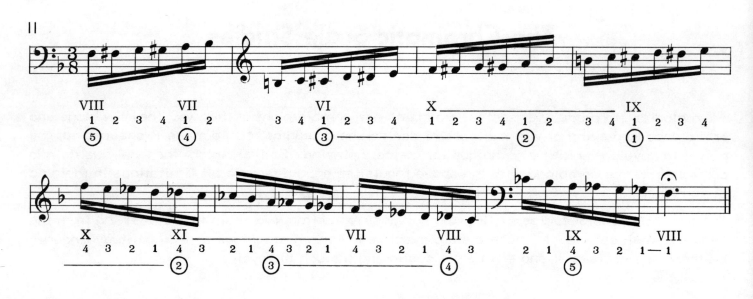

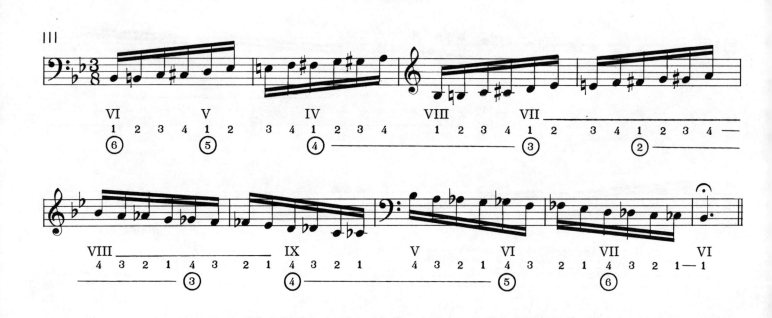

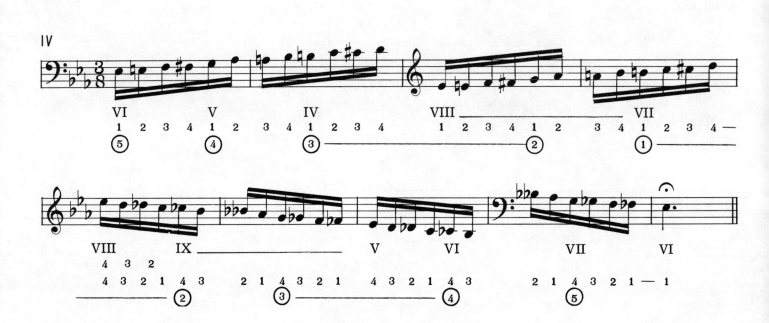

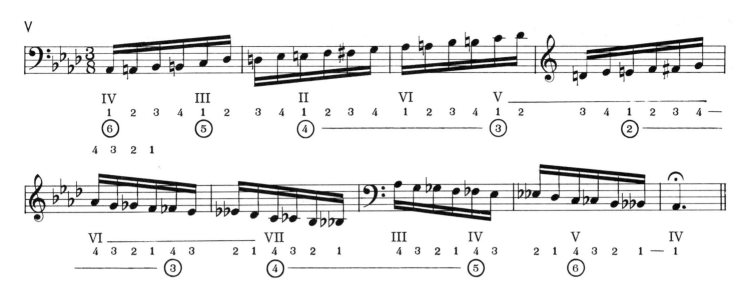

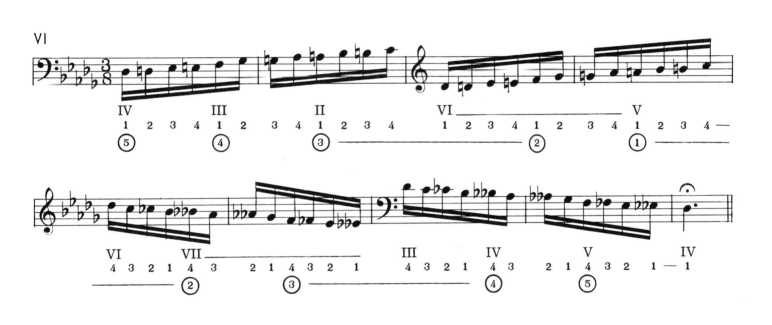

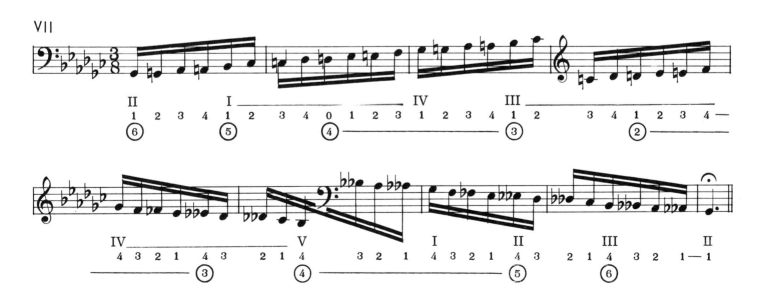

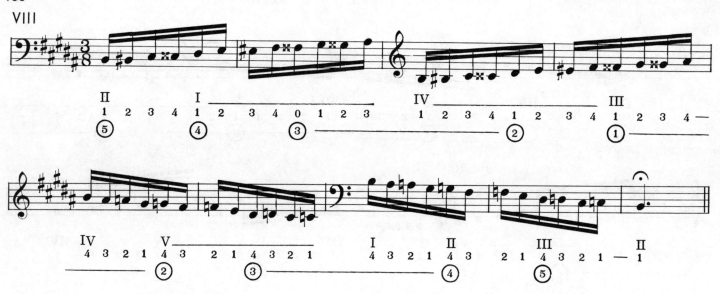

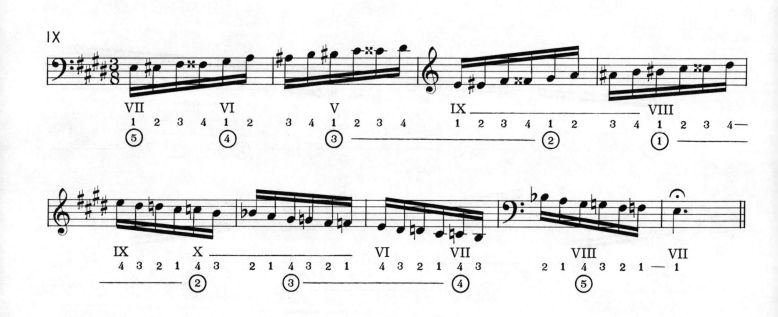

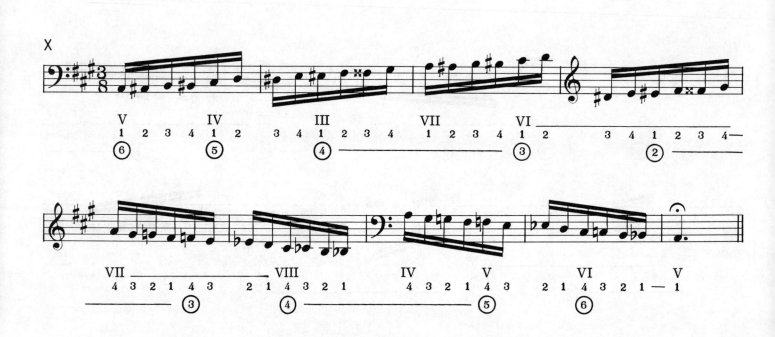

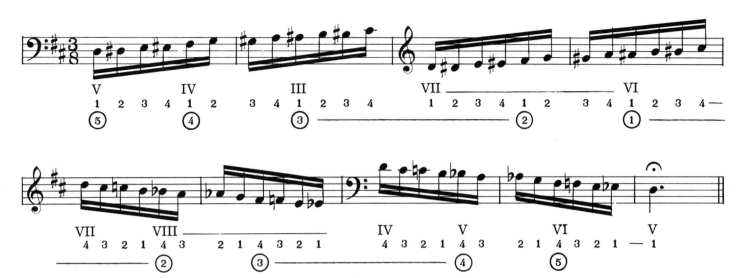

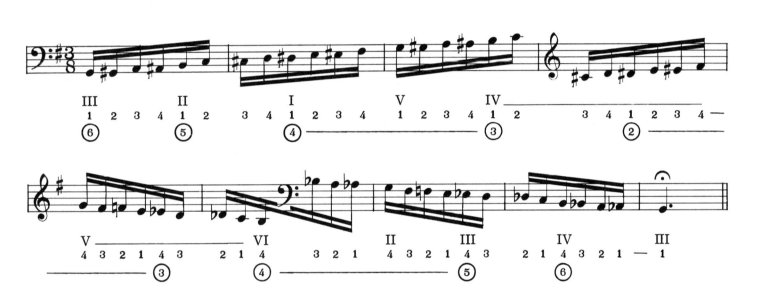

Work out the following supplemental chromatic scale forms:

1. Scale number 1 starting on the ⑥ stg VIII pos.

2. Scale number 6 starting on the ⑥ stg IX pos.

3. Scale number 7 starting on the ⑤ stg IX pos.

4. Scale number 8 starting on the ⑥ stg VII pos.

Supplemental Chromatic Study for the Key of E

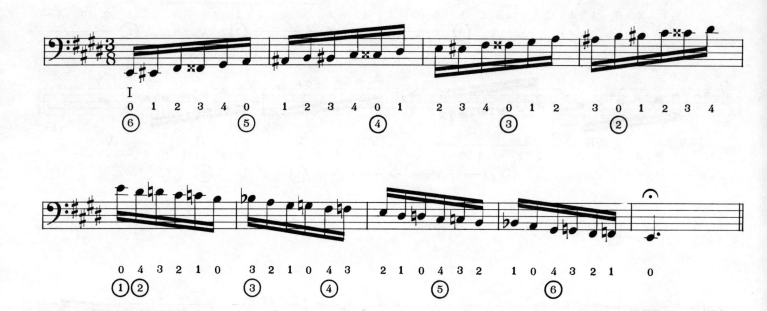

When practicing the chromatic scale studies throughout the cycle, it is advisable to relax for five to ten seconds between each exercise. This will keep the muscles from becoming and remaining tense. Frequent rest periods is advisable when practicing any of the scale and arpeggio studies.

169

The Major Add Nine Chords

The major ADD NINE chord is a major chord with the ninth tone added.

The add nine chord would be structured:

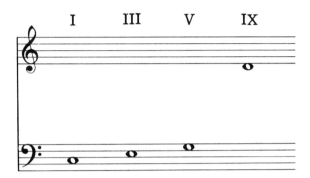

The ninth tone would usually resolve down a whole step to the tonic note of a major chord as given in the following example:

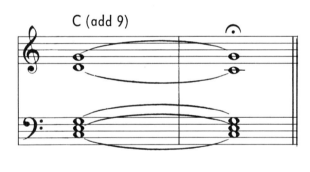

In the example shown, the IX to VIII(D to C) serves as a resolution for the C chord being held for an extended period. The use of such a resolution is prevalent, when the chord is voiced with fifth on top (as in the example shown).

Basic Form Add Nine Chords

I III V IX

Chord symbol example: C(add 9)

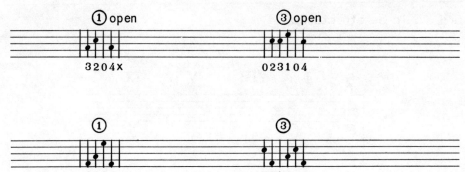

(Practice the "add 9"——▶major resolutions throughout cycle, using most convenient fingering for the major chords)

The Minor Add Nine Chord

The minor add nine chord is used the same as a major add nine but resolving to a minor chord instead of a major chord:

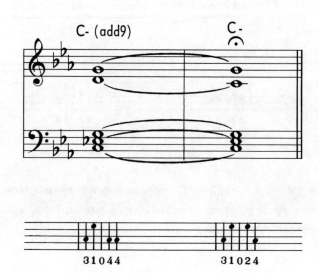

Basic Form Minor Add Nine Chords

I ♭III V IX

Chord symbol example: C- (add 9)

(Practice the minor ("add 9")——▶minor resolutions throughout cycle.)

The Major Six-Nine Chords

The major six-nine chord is a major sixth chord with the ninth tone added and, like the major sixth, is a *nonresolving* chord. It is used quite frequently as a strong closing chord voicing for the end of a phrase of a song. One interesting characteristic of the six-nine chord is the fourth step intervals in the upper structure of the chord when the chord is notated correctly:

Example I

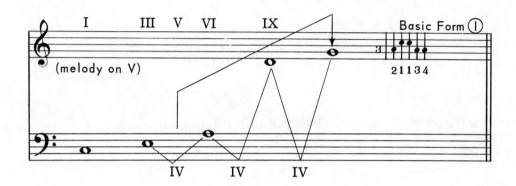

To get a good C $\frac{6}{9}$ voicing instead of (I III V VI IX) the fifth (G) was raised an octave eliminating the whole step spacing of V and VI (G and A). Note the sequence of fouth steps: (E

A D G). In this particular voicing, these notes (not the root) could be moved a fourth step higher, creating a perfect upper structure inversion of this $\frac{6}{9}$ chord. The third (E) could be left in the chord structure or omitted:

Example II

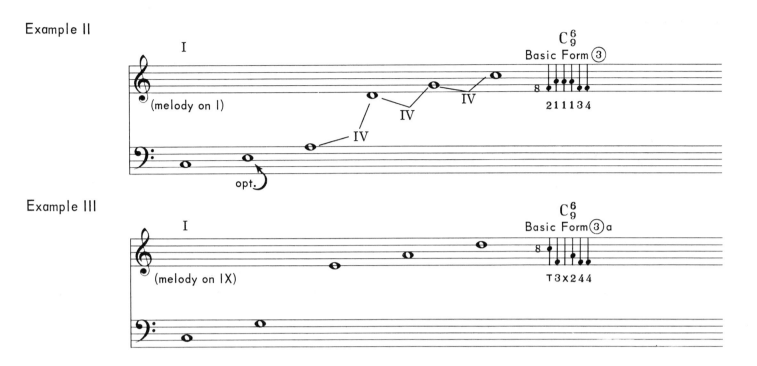

Example III

Because of the inversion potential of the fourth intervals in the upper structure of the $\frac{6}{9}$ chord, the creation of a chord melody can be done simply by using the top three notes of each of the examples shown:

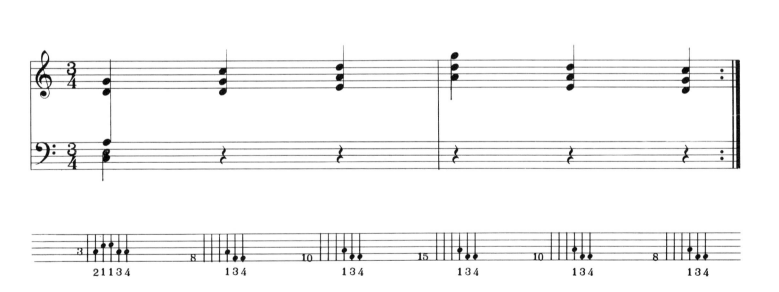

Example IV (melody on III)

The $\frac{6}{9}$ chord voicing can be used when the melody note is on the third of the chord:

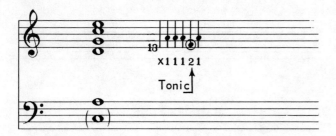

It is not practical to apply this voicing directly to the guitar without deleting the root. When this voicing is needed, the chord can be located by using the note on the second string as the tonic note.

Example V (melody on VI)

Voicing the $\frac{6}{9}$ chord with the sixth tone as the melody note would require deletion of the fifth tone and doubling the sixth:

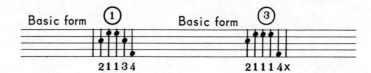

As you can see, the top note (VI) in the above chords is doubled in the lower part of the chord form.

The Minor Six-Nine Chords

The minor six-nine chords are used very similar to the minor sixth chords. Not having equally spaced intervals in the upper structure, (like the major six-nine) the minor six-nine does not have the inversion capabilities of the major six-nine.

Basic Form Minor Six- Nine Chords

I ♭III V VI IX   Chord symbol example: C- $\frac{6}{9}$

The minor six-nine is voiced so as to eliminate the whole step spacing between V and VI (same as the major six-nine)

NOTE: The minor six-nine chord should not be used if the melody note is the tonic note of the chord. This would create the undesirable whole step spacing between IX and VIII.

The Dominant Ninth Chords
(Root Position)

The dominant ninth chord is the extension of the dominant seventh chord and generally resolves the same as a dominant seventh (fourth step). Because of having to delete the third, basic form two will not be used in any basic form ninth chords.

Basic Form Dominant Ninth Chords
(Root Position)

I III V ♭VII IX

Chord symbol example: C9

C9 (Basic resolution to F)

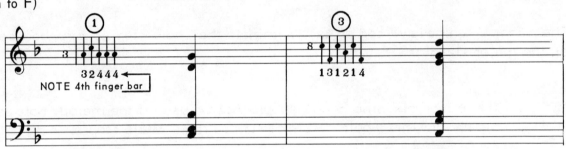

F9 (Basic resolution to B♭)

Bb9 (Basic resolution to Eb)

Eb9 (Basic resolution to Ab)

Ab9 (Basic resolution to Db)

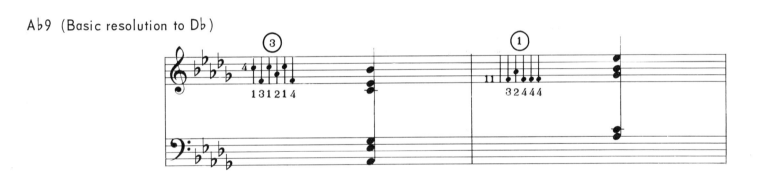

Db9 (Basic resolution to Gb)

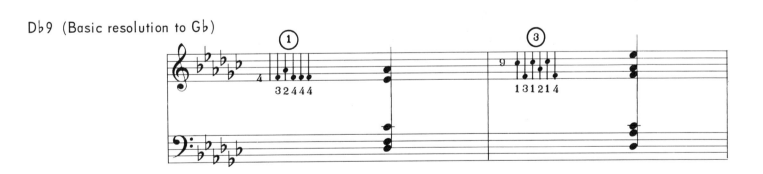

F#9 (Basic resolution to B)

B9 (Basic resolution to E)

E9 (Basic resolution to A)

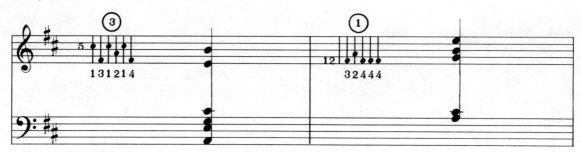

A9 (Basic resolution to D)

D9 (Basic resolution to G)

G9 (Basic resolution to C)

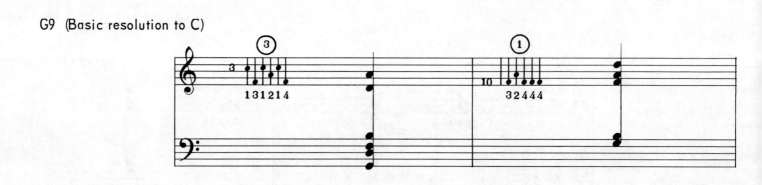

PLAY THIS SEQUENCE FROM MEMORY:

C 9	①	③
F 9	③	①
B♭ 9	③	①
E♭ 9	①	③
A♭ 9	③	①
D♭ 9	①	③
F♯ 9	③	①
B 9	①	③
E 9	③ open	①
A 9	③	①
D 9	①	③
G 9	③	①

Root Inversions of the Dominant Ninth Chord

Example I

Voicing the ninth chords with the third in the bass.

Root on the ⑤ string.

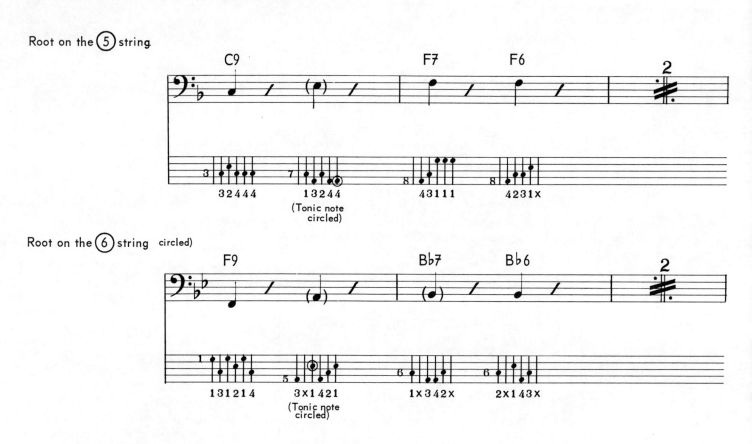

Voicing the ninth with the fifth in the bass, is usually done to accommodate an alternating bass line with the chord remaining the same, however, the ninth chord may be inverted to V in the bass to fit with a diminished chord phrase.

Example II

Voicing the ninth with the fifth in the bass to accommodate an alternating bass line with the chord remaining the same.

With the fifth in the bass of a ninth chord, the root (directly above the fifth) is usually omitted, therefore, these inverted ninth chords will have to be identified and located by the V of the chord.

Example III

Inverting the ninth to the second inversion (V in the bass) to voice in a phrase with diminished chords.

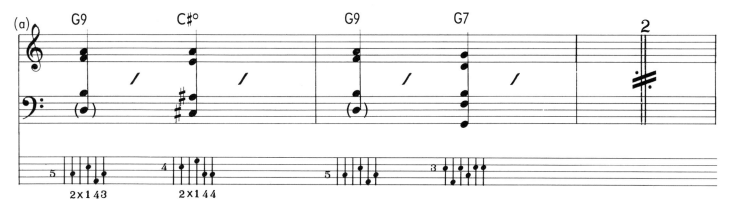

Note that the C#° is named from the bass note and remains a diminished chord even though the melody note (top note 'A') is not a part of a C#° chord.

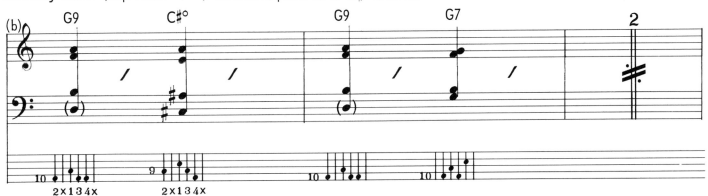

With the diminished chords in a different mode.

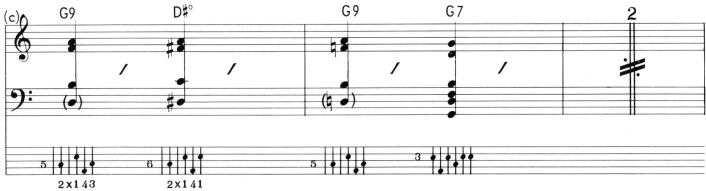

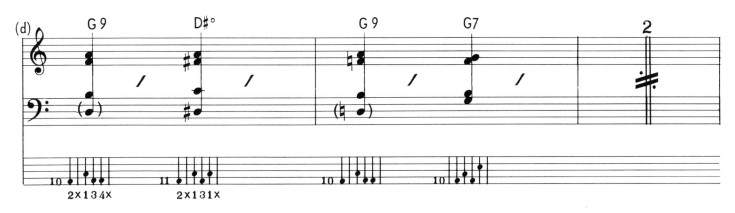

For further upper structure expansions and inversions, review Part I, pages 81-84.

The Augmented Ninth Chords

I III ♭VII +V 1X

Chord symbol example: C+9

(NOTE: The +V has been raised one octave for tonal clarity.)
As the symbol shows, the augmented ninth chord is a dominant ninth with a raised fifth. The augmented ninth usually resolves to a fourth step.

BASIC FORMS

* 21334   TX1234

* Practice to keep the second finger *arched* and not collapsed in the first joint like the third finger.

The following examples show some chord patterns using the augmented ninth chord.

Exercise I (resolving to a major seventh)

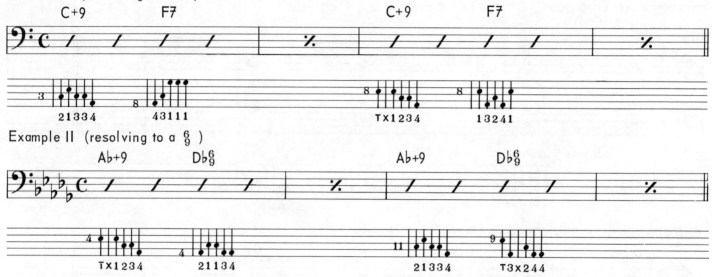

Example II (resolving to a $\frac{6}{9}$)

This example shows the augmented ninth being used in a secondary position and resolving to another augmented ninth:

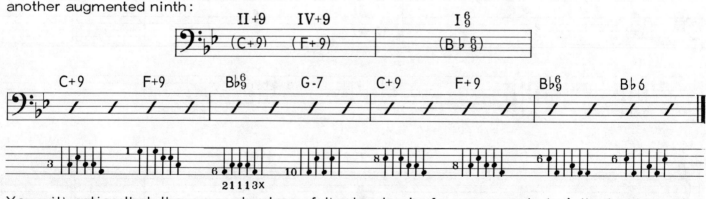

You will notice that the upper structure of the two basic form augmented ninth chords are the same formation. Because of the inverting characteristics of the augmented chords, the upper structure of the augmented chord inverts when moved up or down one half octave.

Example:

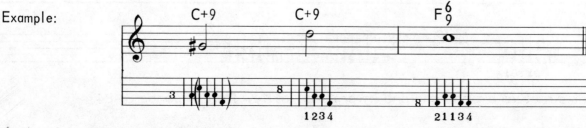

A chordal melody was created by inverting the upper structure of the augmented 9 chord.

Using the Numerical System of Transposition

Similar exercises can be worked out in other keys by using the numerical system of transposition. For example, if you wanted to transpose the preceeding exercise from the key of B♭ to the key of F♯ you could do so by the following method:

STEP I

Number the notes of a B♭ scale, starting with numeral one on B♭.

I	II	III	IV	V	VI	VII
B♭	C	D	E♭	F	G	A

The scale now shows the numerical relationship between each of the notes or chords and the root B♭.

STEP II

Construct a similar scale in the key to be transposed to (In this example, F♯)

I	II	III	IV	V	VI	VII
F♯	G♯	A♯	B	C♯	D♯	E♯

Numerical pattern used in preceeding Example III:

II+9	V+9	I $^6_9$	VI-7	II+9	V+9	I $^6_9$	I 6

STEP III

Fill in root names by looking below each number and note in the new key (F♯). The names of the chords in F♯ would be:

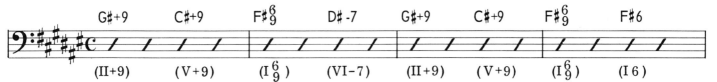

G♯+9	C♯+9	F♯ $^6_9$	D♯ -7	G♯+9	C♯+9	F♯ $^6_9$	F♯6
(II+9)	(V+9)	(I $^6_9$)	(VI-7)	(II+9)	(V+9)	(I $^6_9$)	(I 6)

Accidentals may be used in front of the numerals when working outside the diatonic scale.

Root Inversions of the Augmented Ninth Chords

(1st INVERSION ONLY)

Example:

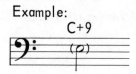

BASIC FORMS

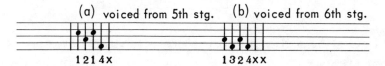

(a) voiced from 5th stg.   (b) voiced from 6th stg.

1 2 1 4 x   1 3 2 4 x x

(Form (b) should be avoided in the lower register)

The following exercises use the inverted augmented ninth chords in a couple of common patterns.

Example I

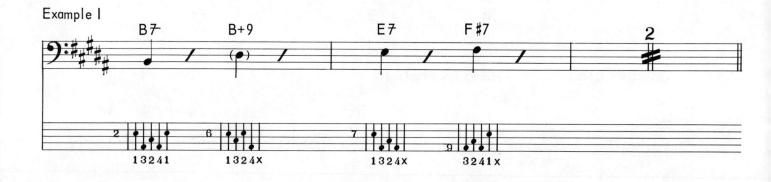

Example II

Alterations of the Dominant Ninth Chords

Because of the dominant ninth chords being extensions of the dominant seventh chords, the altered ninth chords are named as seventh chords with the alteration of the ninth designated. Take for an example, the following chord structure:

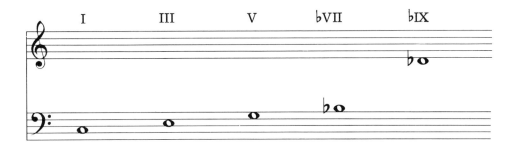

This chord would be called "C seven flat nine" and the chord symbol would be "C7♭9." The same is true when the eleventh is added to the altered ninth chords. Take for an example the following chord structure:

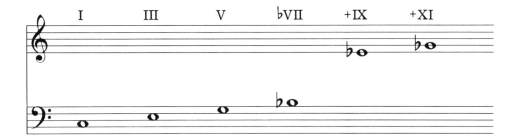

This chord could be called "C seven plus nine plus eleven" and the chord symbol would be "C7+9+11." As you can see, the chord symbol clearly designates the alterations of the ninth and eleventh tones above the dominant seventh chord.

The Basic Form Seven Flat Nine Chords

I III ♭VII ♭IX

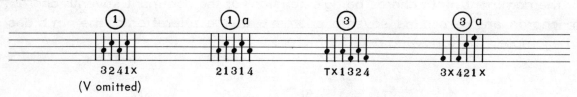

In forms ①a and ③ , the form (C) diminished chord can be easily recognized. A chord melody or fill-in can be created simply by inverting the diminished chord form in the upper structure of the seven flat nine chord.

The following examples show some chord patterns using the seven flat nine chord.

Example I (resolving from IV7♭9 to I7 or I6)

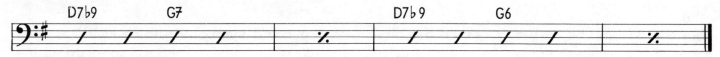

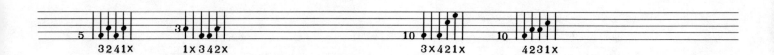

Example II (resolving from III7♭9 to IV7♭9 to I⁶₉)

Example III (resolving from II7♭9 to IV7♭9 to I-)

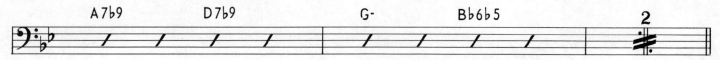

In example II and example III the chromatic motion of the diminished chord in the upper structure of the seven flat nine is easily discernable.

Root Inversions of the Seven Flat Nine Chords

On occasion the seven flat nine chords will be inverted to their first, second and third inversions (III in the bass, V in the bass, and bVII in the bass). All of these inversions are formed the same as the diminished chord forms.

Example I

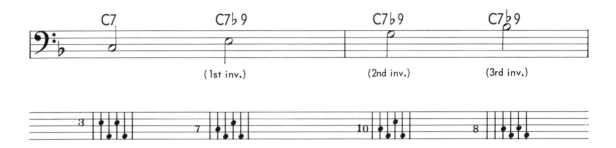

Example II

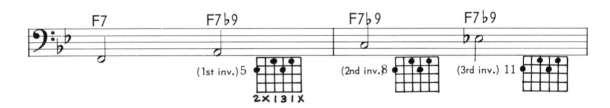

The following examples show the inverted seven flat nine chords used in the most common chord patterns.

Example I (Using V in the bass to get alternating bass notes on the same chord)

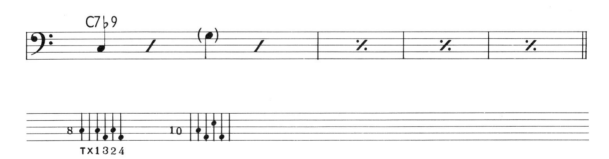

Example II (Using 1st inversion)

2x131x

Attention is called to the half step progression between the *inverted seven flat nine* in bar ① and the *IV major* in bar ② of the above excercises. These half step progressions conform to the rules concerning progressions of the diminished chords themselves.

Example III (Typical phrases using the 3rd inversion of the 7b9 chord.)

2x134x

Example III (Typical phrases using the 3rd inversion of the 7b9 chord.)

2314x

The 7♭9 inversions can be used to relate the diminished chords to the 7♭9 chord, however, the easiest way to establish the diminished chord relative to the 7♭9 is to use the diminished chord root a MAJOR THIRD ABOVE THE ROOT OF THE 7♭9 CHORD. Listed below are examples of these relationships:

C 7♭9   (E°)

F 7♭9   (A°)

B♭7♭9   (D°)

E♭7♭5   (G°)

A♭7♭9   (C°)

D♭7♭9   (F°)

G♭7♭9   (B♭°)

B7 9   (D♯°)

E 7♭9   (G♯°)

A 7♭9   (C♯°)

D 7♭9   (F♯°)

G 7♭9   (B°)

190

These diminished chords may be used as substitutions for the seven flat nine chord, however, discretion should be used in deciding the best one to use. The one that should be avoided is the one that would put the root of the diminished chord on half step above the root of the seven flat nine chord. Example: C7♭9 (D♭°). In reality the D♭, one half step above the root C, would constitute a *FLAT SECOND* instead of a flat nine and should be avoided.

To create a melodic line for a seven flat nine chord, a diminished arpeggio can be used starting from the third above the root of the 7♭9 chord:

If the diminished (8 tone) scale were used, the scale should be determined by starting from the root of the 7♭9 chord. In the following example the descending portion of the diminished scale is used:

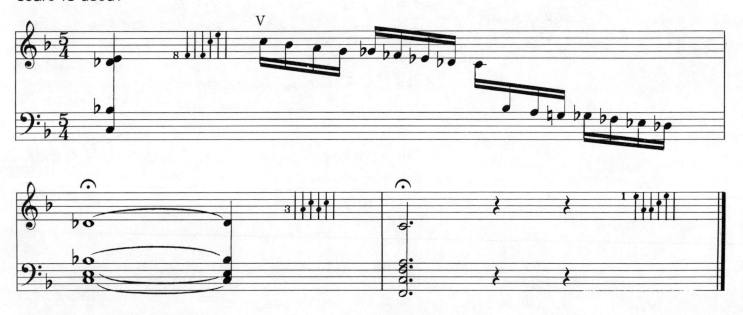

As mentioned previously, chromatic movement of the diminished chords (usually descending) can be used when progressing from 7♭9 to 7♭9 in fourth steps:

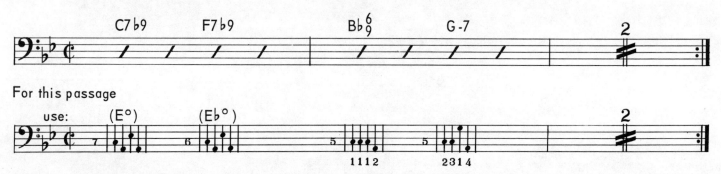

For this passage

Parallel chromatic motion can be used in many instances when fourth step progressions are used, and other examples will be studied with other chords.

The Dominant Ninth Flat Five Chords

I III ♭V ♭VII IX   Chord symbol example: C9♭5

BASIC FORMS

21341   TX2314

Voicing the flat five above the ninth in form one gives the chord the appearance of an eleventh chord.   If the flat five were voiced below the ninth in form one, the third would be sacrificed:

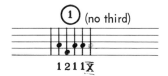

1211X̱

In the subsequent study of the eleventh chords the same form will be used for form one eleventh. The major difference between the two chords will be noted in the fact that the eleventh chord has the *natural five* and the *raised eleventh* (octave +IV which is one octave above the flat five). As you will note, the 9♭5 *does not* have a natural five.

The most frequent use of the 9♭5 chord is to accommodate a melodic line, as shown in the following examples:

Example I

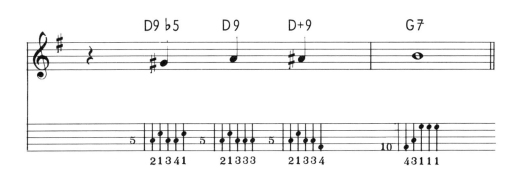

21341   21333   21334   43111

Example II

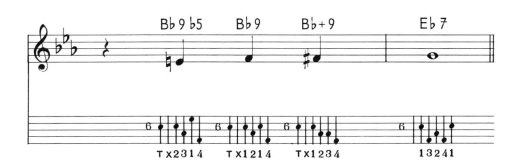

TX2314   TX1214   TX1234   13241

The Seven Flat Nine Flat Five Chords

I   III ♭V ♭VII ♭IX   Chord symbol example: C7♭9♭5

BASIC FORMS

The most common resolution for the 7♭9♭5 chord is to a fourth step:

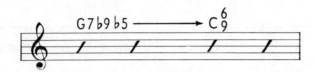

The 7♭9♭5 chord is also one of the chords that the upper structure can be moved chromatically down if the bass line progresses in fourth steps:

Example I

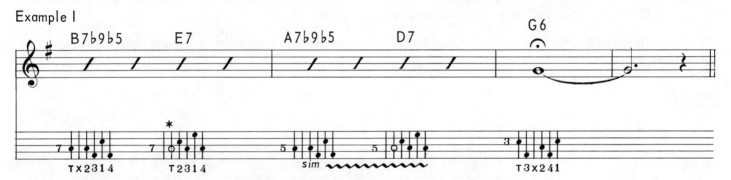

Noting with the thumb on the fifth string is very difficult and can be deleted. The location of the root of the chord is circled.

Example II

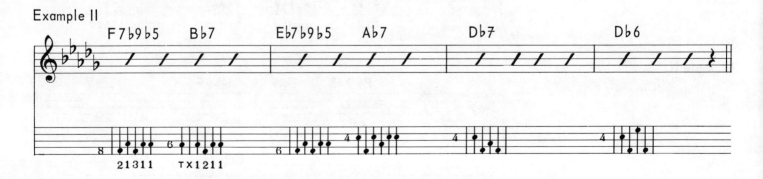

Work similar exercises throughout the cycle using numerical transposition.

Attention should be called to the OUTSIDE FORMS (a) and (c) of the dominant seventh inversions (Part I, pg. 93). Because of the polytonic nature of the 7♭9♭5 chord, root inversions are *not used*.

The Augmented Seventh Flat Nine Chords

I III ♭VII ♭IX + V   Chord symbol example: C+7(♭9)

NOTE: The recommended structuring of the +7(♭9) is to voice the +V one octave higher
as shown.

BASIC FORMS

The most common resolution for the +7♭9 chord is a IV 9 or IV⁶₉ . The upper structure can be
moved chromatically down with a fourth step bass line, creating the following pattern:

Some typical phrases using the +7♭9 chord are shown in the following examples:

Example I

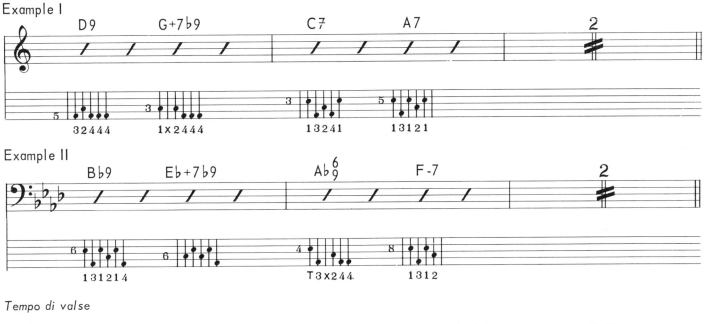

Example II

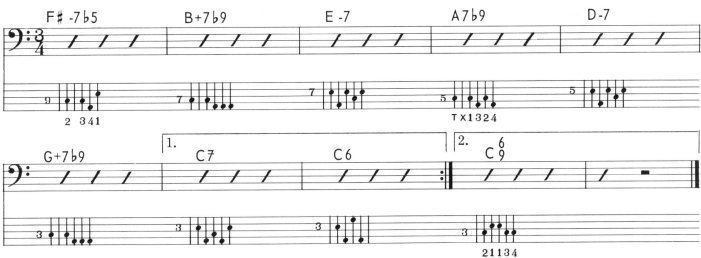

Root Inversions of the Augmented Seventh Flat Nine Chords

(1st INVERSION ONLY)

BASIC FORMS
(III in the bass)

The root and tonic notes are deleted from these forms and the chords will have to be identified by one of the intervals of the chords:

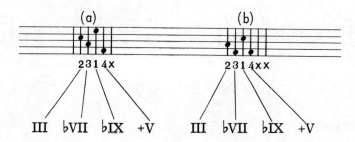

The simplest method, by far, is locating the chord by the bass note as shown in the following phrases:

Example I

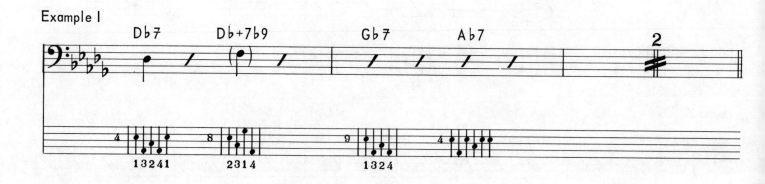

Example II

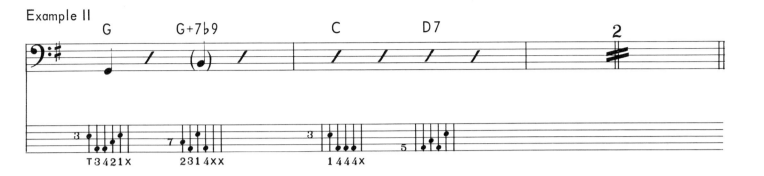

Example III

The following exercise uses the +7♭9 in a descending pattern and changing to a different chord when moved a half step lower:

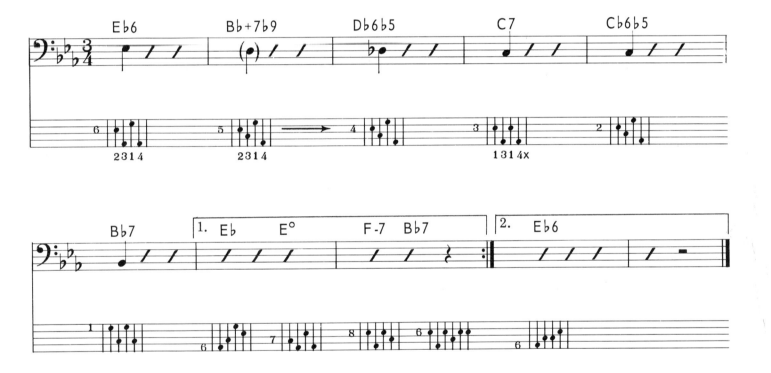

Example IV

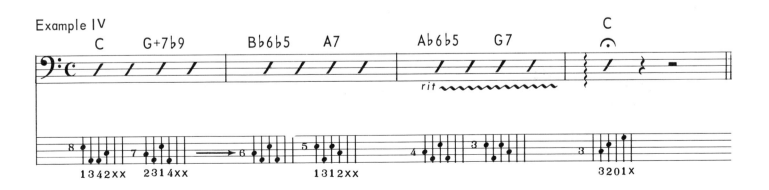

The Seventh Raised Nine Chords

I   III   V   bVII   +IX   Chord symbol example: C7(+9)

BASIC FORMS

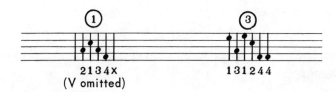

The raised ninth interval, being the octave minor third, is used extensively in jazz music to establish a minor mode. It is also used frequently as an ending chord of a song. The following examples are some of the common ways in which the 7(+9) chords are used:

Example I

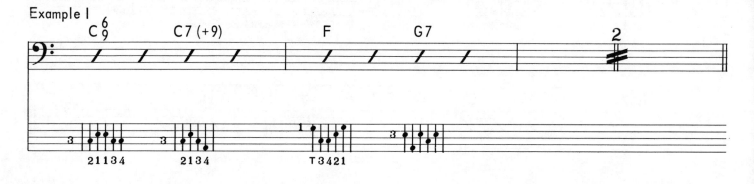

Example II

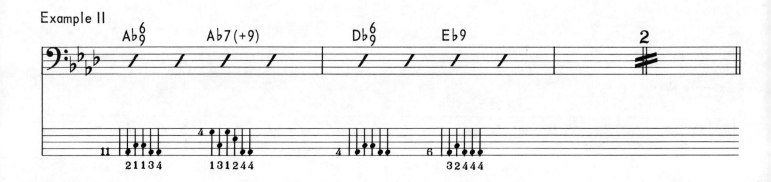

Inverting the Seventh Raised Nine Chords

(1st INVERSION ONLY)

BASIC FORMS

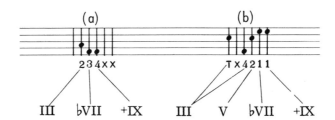

(These chords should be identified by the third in the bass.)

Typical phrases using the inverted 7(+9) chords:

Example I

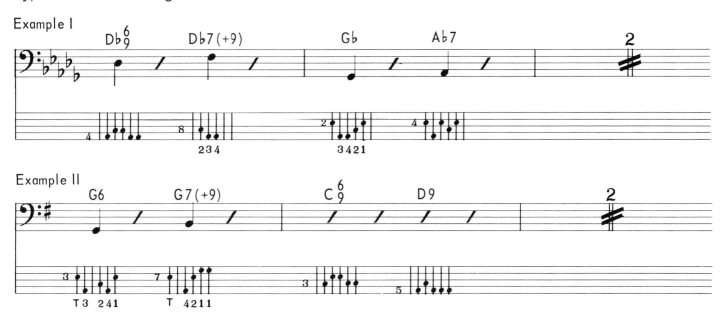

Example II

Another common phrase using the 7(+9):

(II9 ⟶ bII 7(+9) ⟶ I$^6_9$)

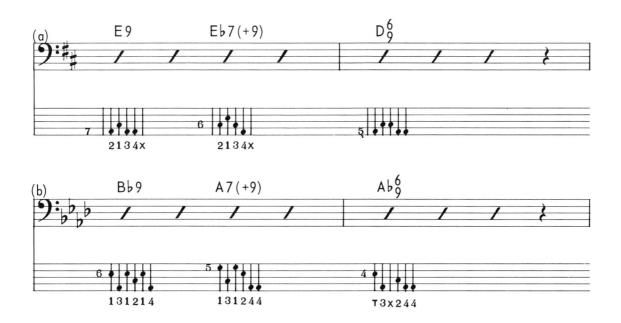

The next examples show the 7(+9) being used as the final chord of a song:

Example I

Example II

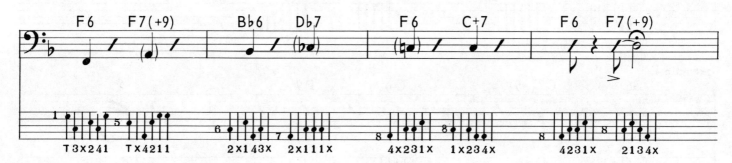

The eight tone scale will create a melodic line to fit the seven raised nine chord.
(Review page 35)

The Augmented Seventh Raised Nine Chords

I   III ∟bVII +V +IX

Chord symbol example: C+7 (+9)

NOTE: The recommended structuring of the +7(+9) is to voice the +V one octave higher as shown.

BASIC FORMS

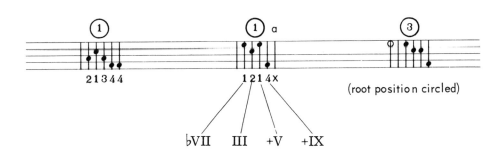

21344   1214x

(root position circled)

bVII   III   +V   +IX

The root is deleted in form ① a and is not practical in form ③ . Form ① a should only be used in the higher positions and located by the bVII in the bass. The most common phrase using the +7(+9) is following a 13th chord: ($II^{13} \longrightarrow V+7(+9) \longrightarrow I^6_9$)

The following exercises will use the 13th chord even though the study of the 13th chords comes later in this text.

200

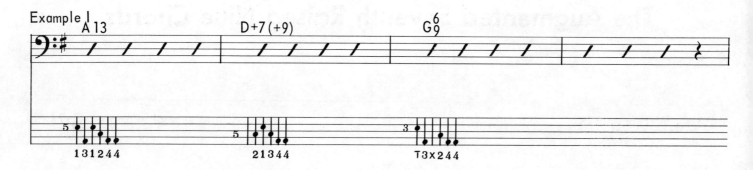

The chromatic motion in the upper structure of the chords in these exercises can be clearly recognized.

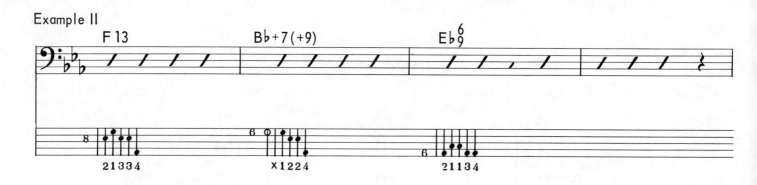

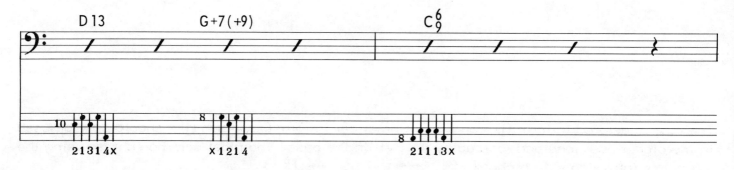

The Minor Ninth Chords

(Root Position)

The minor ninth chord is the extension of the minor seventh chord and usually resolves the same way as the minor seventh (IV 7).

Basic Form Minor Ninth Chords

(Root Position)

I ♭III V ♭VII IX   Chord symbol example: C -9

C -9 (Basic resolution to F 7)

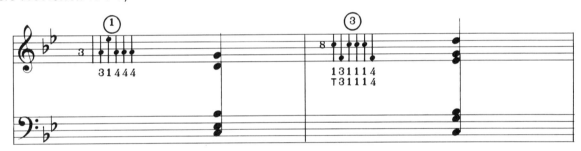

F -9 (Basic resolution to B♭ 7)

B♭ -9 (Basic resolution to E♭ 7)

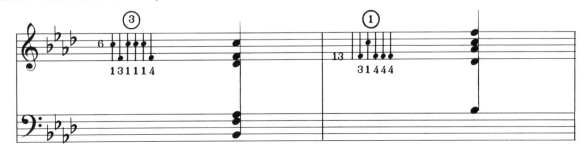

Eb-9 (Basic resolution to Ab7)

Ab-9 (Basic resolution to Db7)

C#-9 (Basic resolution to F#7)

F#-9 (Basic resolution to B7)

B-9 (Basic resolution to E7)

E-9 (Basic resolution to A 7)

A-9 (Basic resolution to D 7)

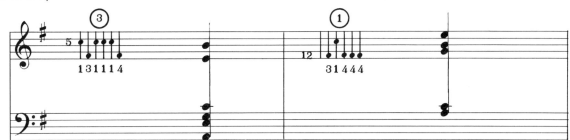

D-9 (Basic resolution to G 7)

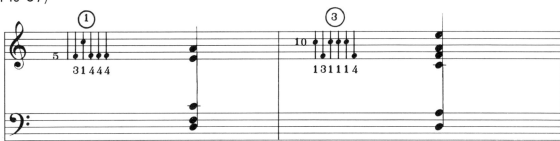

G-9 (Basic resolution to C 7)

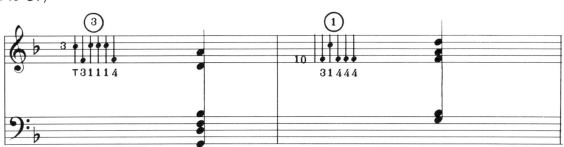

MEMORIZE THIS SEQUENCE

C −9	①	③		F♯ −9	③	①
F −9	③	①		B −9	① open	③
B♭ −9	③	①		E −9	③ open ③ a	①
E♭ −9	①	③		A −9	③	①
A♭ −9	③	①		D −9	①	③
C♯ −9	①	③		G −9	③	①

Two of the most common phrases using the minor ninth chord are used in the following
exercise.

$$(II-9 \longrightarrow V7 \longrightarrow I\bar{7} \longrightarrow I6 \longrightarrow II-9 \longrightarrow bII9 \longrightarrow I\,{}^{6}_{9}\,)$$

Work this exercise out to where it can be played entirely without interruption. Use chord forms
of your choice.

NOTE: Some interesting melodic and chordal ideas can be accomplished by using the minor
triad in the upper structure of the minor ninth chord as a simple component to work with.

Root Inversions of the Minor Ninth Chords

 1st INVERSION (♭3rd in the bass)

As it works out, the first inversion of the minor ninth chord will be one of the basic form major seventh chords.

Example:

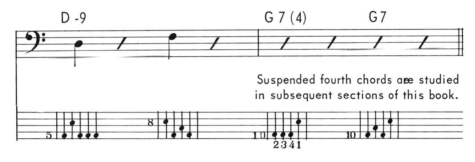

These are intervals of the C -9 and not the (E♭7).

Situations calling for an inversion of the minor ninth chord are not too common, however, the following examples show the most likely type of phrase that would be ussd.

Example I

Suspended fourth chords are studied in subsequent sections of this book.

Example II

Using the pattern (II-9 ——→ II-9 ——→ V 7 (4) ——→ V 7) work similar exercises throughout cycle.
(♭III)

2nd INVERSION (5th in the bass)

The second inversion would usually be used in an alternating bass situation. Deleting the root on the sixth string of form ③ would give the correct 2nd inversion voicing.

For form ①, it would be advisable to delete the root (directly above the V) from the chord form:

If an alternating bass were called for, the third finger can alternate from I to V on the fifth and sixth string as shown in the following exercise:

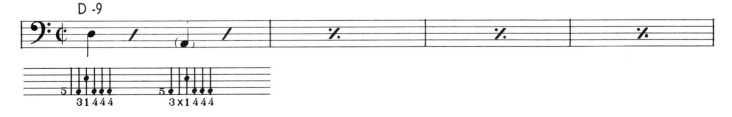

The Major Ninth Chords
(Root Position)

The major ninth chord is the extension of the major seventh chord and like the major seventh, usually resolves to a major sixth or six/nine chord. It is one of the most beautiful of all the chords and some of the interesting aspects of the chord will be studied.

Basic Form Major Ninth Chords

I   III   V   ♮VII   IX   Chord symbol example: Cmaj9 or C9

C9 (Basic resolution to C6)

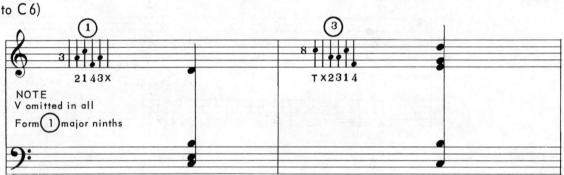

NOTE
V omitted in all
Form ① major ninths

F9 (Basic resolution to F6)

Bb9 (Basic resolution)to Bb6)

Eb9 (Basic resolution to Eb6)

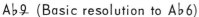

Ab9 (Basic resolution to Ab6)

Db9 (Basic resolution to Db6)

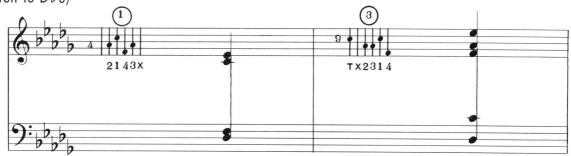

Gb9 (Basic resolution to Gb6)

B9 (Basic resolution to B6)

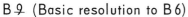

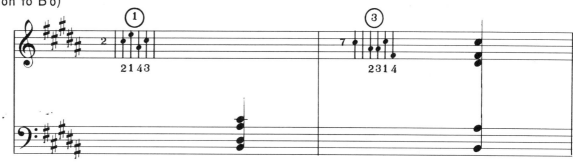

208

E ♀ (Basic resolution to E 6)

031204   023140   2143X

(Pracrice this sequence)

A ♀ (Basic resolution to A 6)

T X2314   2143X

D ♀ (Basic resolution to D 6)

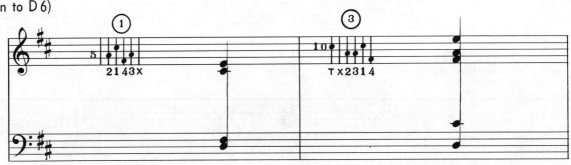

2143X   T X2314

G ♀ (Basic resolution to G 6)

T X2314   2143X

MEMORIZE THE FOLLOWING SEQUENCE

C ♀	①	③
F ♀	③	①
B♭ ♀	③	①
E♭ ♀	①	③
A♭ ♀	③	①
D♭ ♀	①	③
G♭ ♀	③	①
B ♀	①	③
E ♀	③ open	①
A ♀	③	①
D ♀	①	③
G ♀	③	①

Root Inversions of the Major Ninth Chords

1st INVERSION (3rd in the bass)

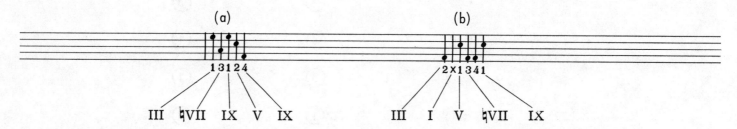

The following examples are two types of phrase using the inverted major ninth chord.

Example I

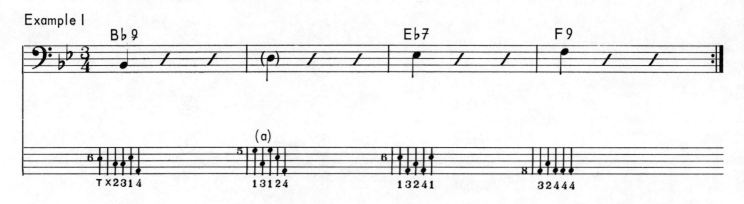

Example II

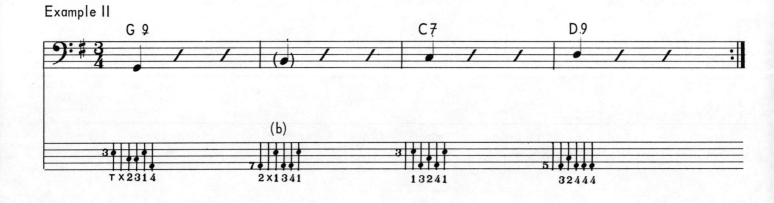

Example III

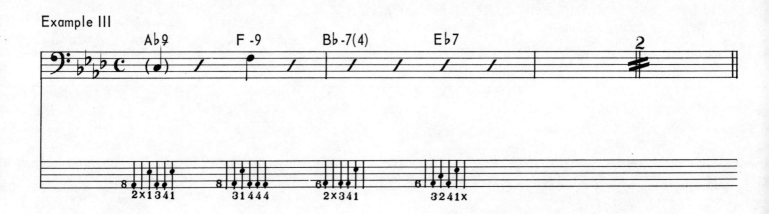

The following examples show the inverted major ninth resolving one-half step lower to a diminished chord.

Example I

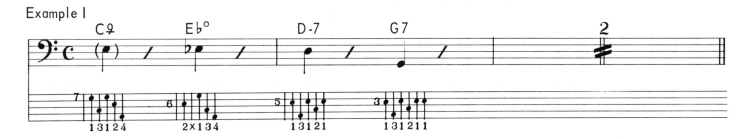

There are melodic situations that would permit the use of the unusual harmonizations shown in Example II although they are rare.

Example II

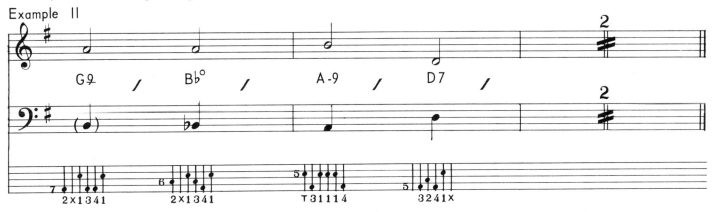

Form ① can be inverted to the second inversion by moving the second finger from the fifth to the sixth string:

Example I

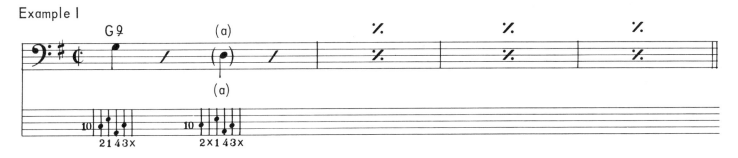

Inverting form ③ to a second inversion is not quite so simple and this exercise should be practiced until it can be played at varying speeds.

Example II

Utilization of the Upper Structure Component of the Major Ninth Chord

You can recognize the outside form (a) of the major sixth inversions (Part I, pg. 104) in the upper structure of the form 3 . Other than the INSIDE FORM (c) and OUTSIDE FORM (b), the major sixth inversions can be used to great advantage when working with the major ninth chords. The use of the inside form (c) and the outside form (b) is not recommended because of creating a II interval by having the ninth tone inverted 8 VB (one octave below). For rhythm and accompaniment, the inside sixth inversions (other than form c) can be used very effectively. The following three examples show the sixth inversions being substituted for the major ninth and also gives examples of the major ninth to sixth resolutions (the root notes are deleted).

Example I

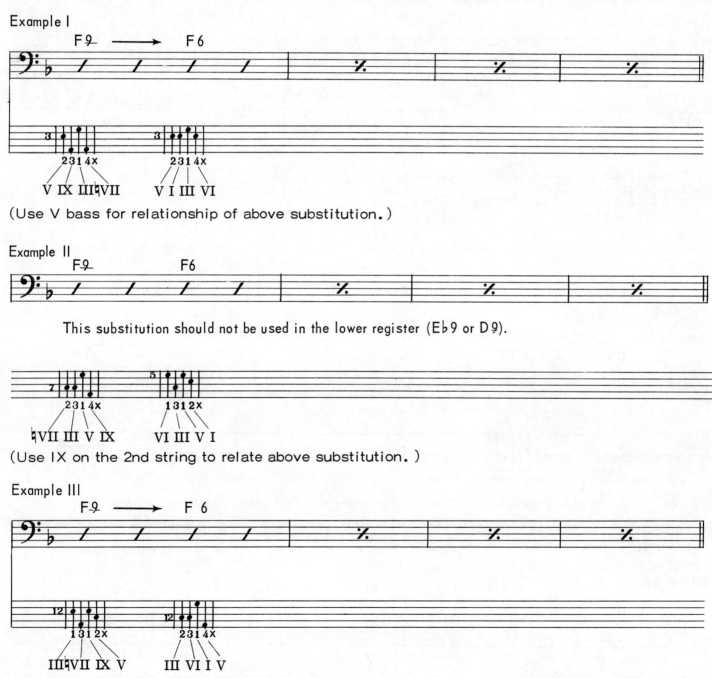

(Use V bass for relationship of above substitution.)

Example II

This substitution should not be used in the lower register (Eb9 or D9).

(Use IX on the 2nd string to relate above substitution.)

Example III

(Use III bass to relate above substitution.)

An easy way of identifying the sixth chord substitution of a major ninth is to relate it to the fifth interval. For example:

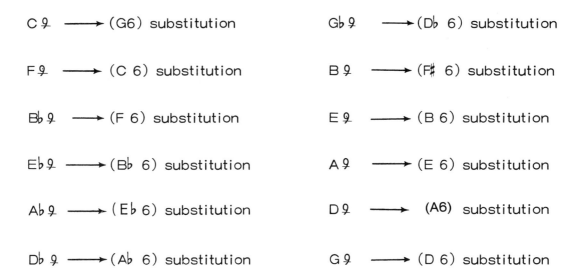

C9 ⟶ (G6) substitution   G♭9 ⟶ (D♭ 6) substitution

F9 ⟶ (C 6) substitution   B9 ⟶ (F♯ 6) substitution

B♭9 ⟶ (F 6) substitution   E9 ⟶ (B 6) substitution

E♭9 ⟶ (B♭ 6) substitution   A9 ⟶ (E 6) substitution

A♭9 ⟶ (E♭ 6) substitution   D9 ⟶ (A6) substitution

D♭9 ⟶ (A♭ 6) substitution   G9 ⟶ (D 6) substitution

The major sixth substitutions can be highly effective when utilized with an extended pattern such as the following examples:

Example I

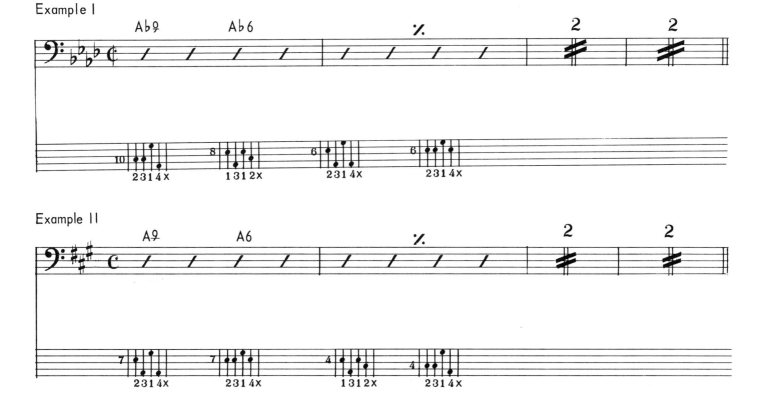

Example II

The outside major sixth inversions are very effective for creating chordal melodies to use with the major ninth chords. Take the following phrase for example:

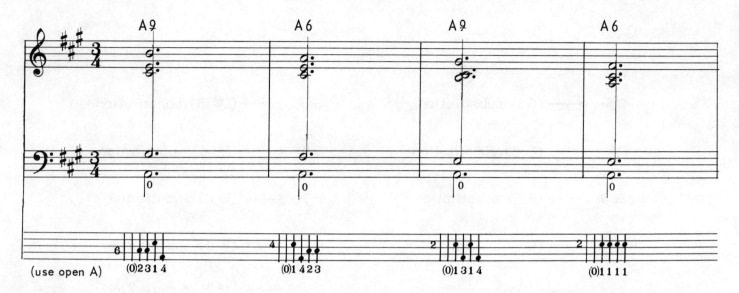

Some of the most interesting and beautiful chordal phrases can be created through experimentation such as the following extended phrase:

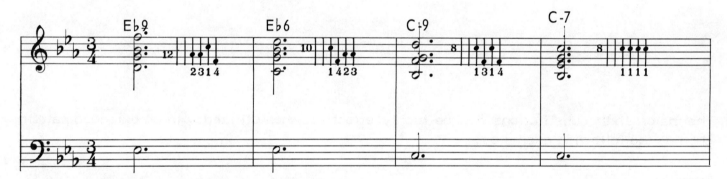

(2nd guitar play bass notes and rhythm)

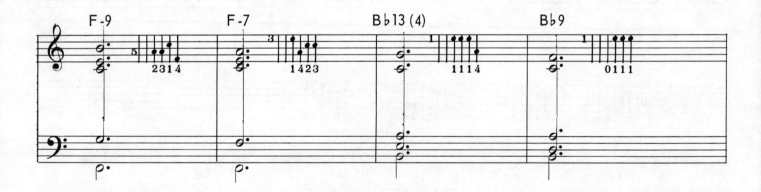

This type of pattern can be used as an introduction to a song very effectively.

There are countless ways that the major sixth substitutions can be used with the major ninth chords as well as with melodic lines. Similar patterns can be worked out using the upper structure inversions of many other chords, such as the dominant ninths/minor sixth inversions (Part I, pg. 80). Studies like these, open up a lifetime of successful experimentation for the serious musician.

The Minor Nine Natural Seven Chords
(Root Position)

The minor nine natural seven chord is the extension of the minor natural seven chord. It's resolution, like the minor natural seven, is to a minor sixth chord.

BASIC FORMS

I bIII V ♮VII IX

Chord symbol example: C-9 (♮7) or C-9

C-9 (Basic resolution to C 6)

F-9 (Basic resolution to C 6)

Bb-9 (Basic resolution to Bb 6)

216

E♭-9 (Basic resolution to E♭-6)

(not to be used for rhythm)

G♯-9 (Basic resolution to G♯-6)

C♯-9 (Basic resolution to C♯-6)

F♯-9 (Basic resolution to F♯-6)

B -9 (Basic resolution to B -6)

E -9 (Basic resolution to E -6)

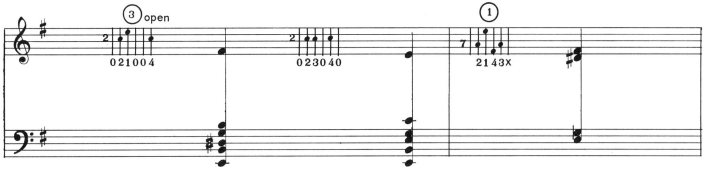

(Practice this sequence)

A -9 (Basic resolution to A -6)

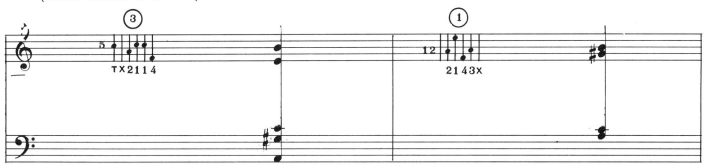

D -9 (Basic resolution to D -6)

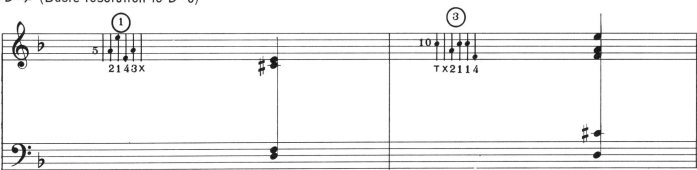

G -9 (Basic resolution to G -6)

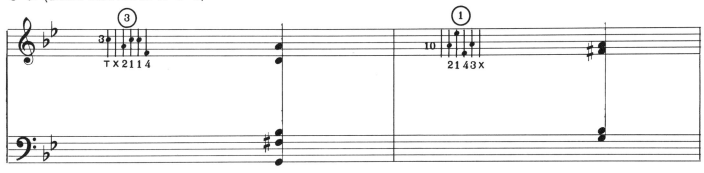

218

MEMORIZE THE FOLLOWING SEQUENCE

C - ♪	①	③	C♯ - ♪	①	③
F - ♪	③	①	F♯ - ♪	③	①
B♭ - ♪	③	①	B - ♪	① open	③
E♭ - ♪	①	③	E - ♪	③ open	①
A♭ - ♪	③	①	A - ♪	③	①
E♭ - ♪	①	③	D - ♪	①	③
G♯ - ♪	③	①	G - ♪	③	①

The following exercises are typical phrases using the minor nine natural seven chord:

Example I

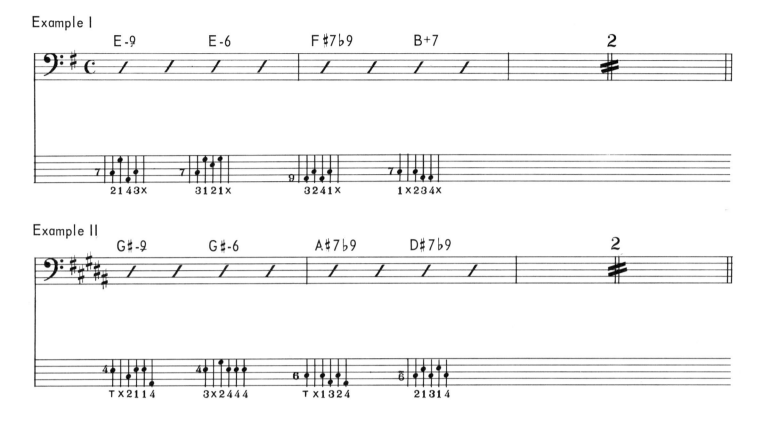

The following exercise uses a very effective substitute for the form ①-9 and the ①-6 chord but should not be used in lower positions (below E-9)

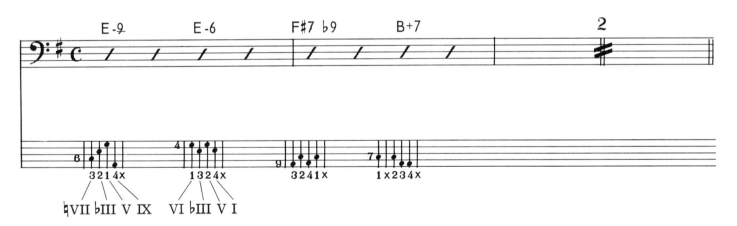

The Suspended Fourth Chords

The fourth suspension is used most frequently with the following chords:

1. MAJOR

2. MINOR

3. DOM. 7th

4. MINOR 7th

5. DOM. 9th

6. THIRTEENTH

In rare cases the suspended fourth will be designated with the minor ninth but, in the pure voicing of a minor ninth (sus. 4) the minor third would be deleted from the chord. To avoid sacrificing the minor third, the fourth tone would be raised one octave and the chord would then be a *minor eleventh*. No example of a minor ninth (sus. 4) progression will be given.

The Major (sus4) Chords

The major chord with a suspended fourth is usually used in the closing phrase of a song and is quite often referred to as a *CHURCH ENDING* because of the frequent use of this type of ending in religious music.

The most common phrase of this type is shown in Example I:

Example I

The following examples are phrases using the major (sus. 4) chord.

Example II

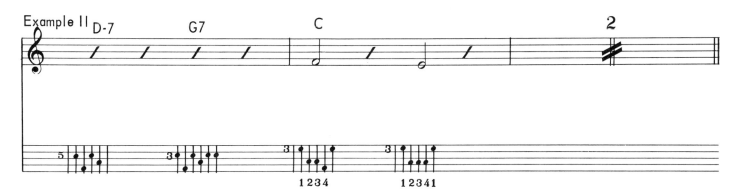

Example II shows the "sus. 4" being indicated by notation rather than by a chord symbol. An important fact to keep in mind is the *OMISSION OF THE MAJOR THIRD WHEN THE FOURTH IS SUSPENDED.*

Example III

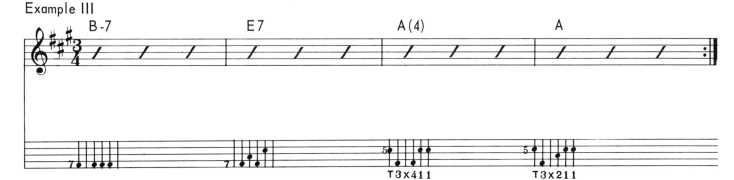

Example IV

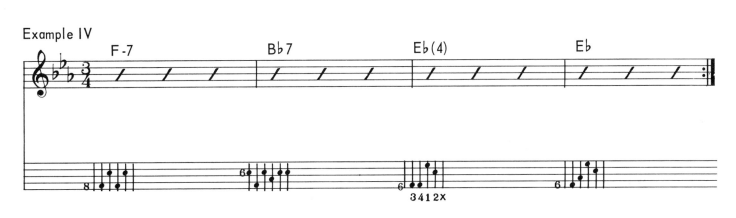

The Minor (sus4) Chords

When the "sus. 4" is used with a minor chord the *MINOR THIRD IS OMITTED* the same as the major third in the major "sus. 4."

The following examples show the sus. 4 being used with minor chords. Because of the thirds being omitted from the suspended major and minor chords, you will note that the sus. 4 chord forms are the same for both major and minor chords.

Example I

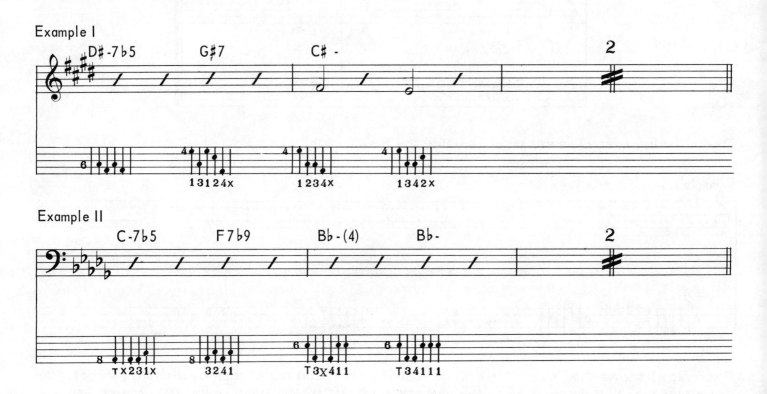

Example III shows the suspended fourth being used in a secondary position and combined with the inversion of some of the other chords to form a melodic continuation of the bass line.

Example III

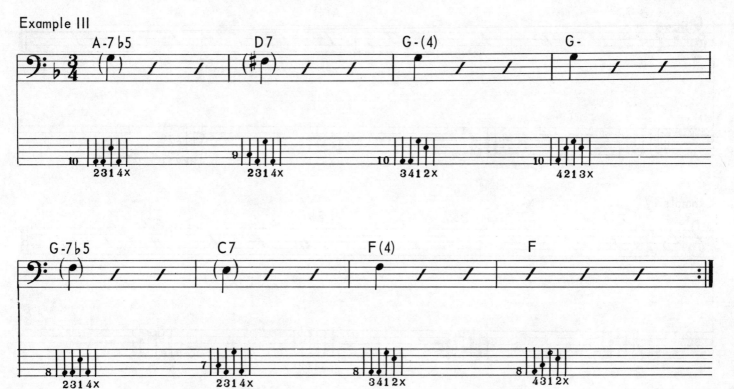

The Dominant Seventh (sus4) Chords

One of the most common ways to expand a simple harmonic pattern is to preceed the dominant seventh chords with a dominant seventh, sus. 4 chord

Take this phraze as example:

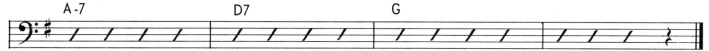

To expand this phrase the dominant 7th can be moved to the second half of the measure and preceeded by a 7 (4) chord:

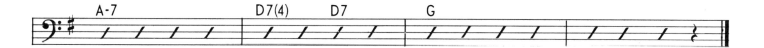

This can be done in most instances provided the MELODY NOTE IS NOT THE *THIRD* OF THE SEVENTH CHORD. If the melody note is the third of the seventh chord, the 4th would create an undesirable half step interval.

Basic Form Seventh (sus4) Chords

Chord symbol example: C7(4)

The most common resolution of the seventh, sus. 4 is resolving the IV to III.

Example:

The following examples show some of the typical patterns using the seventh, sus. 4 chords.

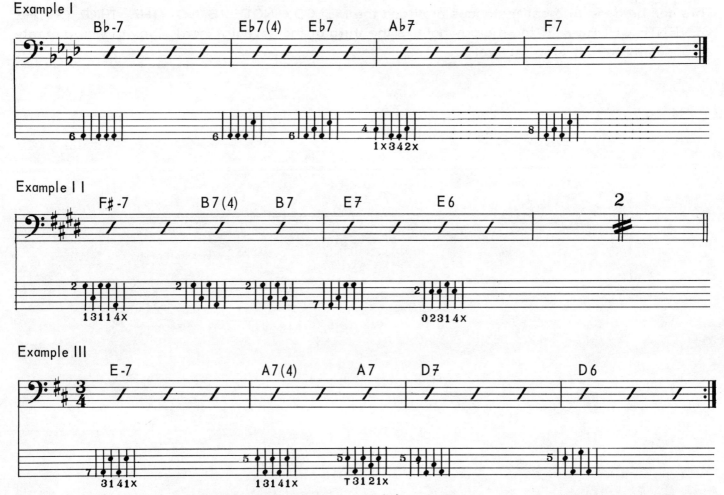

Note in example III the upper structure of the A7(4) is the same as the E-7 chord. Note also that **under no circumstances** would the A7(4) be called E-7(4) - A being the fourth of E.

The Minor Seventh (sus4) Chords

chord symbol example: C-7(4)

The most common resolution of a minor seventh (sus. 4) is to a IV 7 or a IV 7 (4) chord:

Basic Form Minor Seventh (sus4) Chords

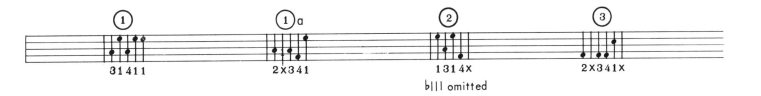

bIII omitted

Because of the whole tone space between the minor third and the fourth, both minor third and fourth are used in the minor seventh (sus. 4).

The following examples use the minor seventh (sus. 4) in some commonly used chord patterns:

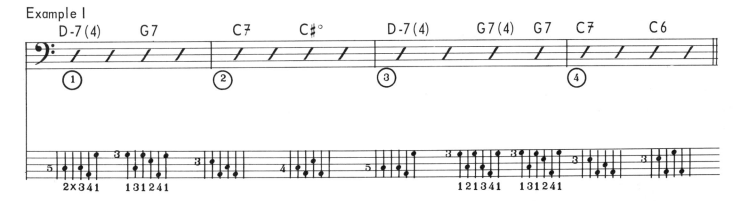

Note the upper structure similarity of the D-7 (4) and the G7 (4) in bar ③. The G7 (4) *WOULD NOT* be called a D-7 (4) with the fourth in the bass.

Example II

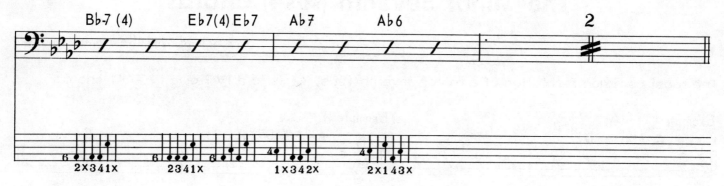

Example III (Min 7 (4) resolving to 7♭5)

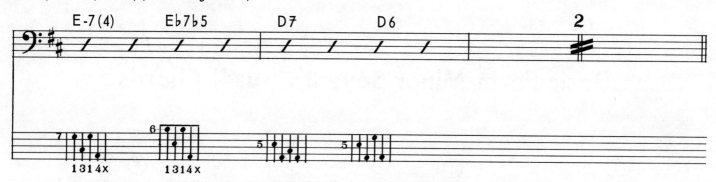

Example IV

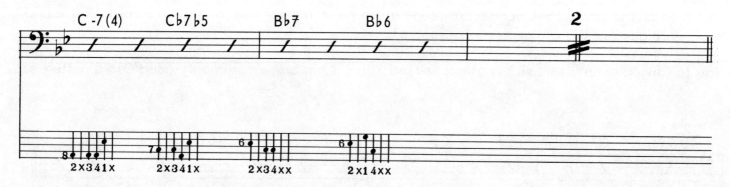

Simplification of the fingering pattern in Example IV was made possible by the deletion of the lesser important notes in the B♭7 and B♭6. By working out connecting fingerings, such as was done in this example, a secondary melody was also created:

The Dominant Ninth (sus4) Chord

Basic resolution to: l9 or l7

Chord symbol example: C 9 (4)

BASIC FORMS

The (34444) fingering would make it easy to resolve the form one C9 (4) to the form one C9 which would be the most commonly used progression. The resolutions for the basic form 9 (4) chords should be practiced throughout the entire cycle.

Looking at the upper structure of the 9 (4) chords you will note one of the sixth/minor seventh inversions studied in Part I, page   (outside forms "a" and "d").

These inversions can be used very effectively in creating a chordal melody to fit the 9 (4) chord.

Voicing the Major and Minor Chords with a Fourth Step (eleventh) Melody

Some of the most beautiful and lasting songs (standards) are songs that make use of the fourth step melody. Two examples of such songs would be:

1. OH! WHAT A BEAUTIFUL MORNING   (Rodgers-Hammerstein)

2. MOON RIVER   (Mancini)

The following examples show a major chord indicated with a fourth step melody.

Example I (♮IV)

Example II (+IV)

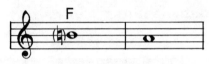

The third example shows a minor chord indicated with a fourth step melody.

Example III (♮IV)

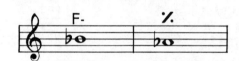

The (+IV) melody would not commonly be used with a minor chord.

The following example shows the creation of a chordal melody to fit the 9 (4) chord and it's resolution:

There is no substitution of chords involved in the above example for only the upper structure of the chord was inverted.

If the inside 6th/minor 7th inversions are used, there should be *at least* a fourth interval *above* the root.

Example   C9(4)

Only forms (c) and (d) should be used, as both forms (a) and (b) would have the lower note a whole step away from the root 'C.'

Unless voiced correctly, the major and minor chord is not a desirable harmonization with a fourth step melody for two reasons:

    1. The fourth step melody creates and open interval. In other words the melody is not harmonized by a third or minor third interval.

    2. The fourth step melody (natural or raised) cancels out the third or minor third of the major or minor chord and therefore the chord is not complete.

The following examples depict undesirable voicings of the major and minor chords with a fourth step melody:

Example I (♮IV)

Example II (+IV)

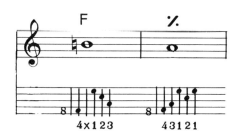

Example III (minor)

In all three examples shown, the fourth or raised fourth melody creates an unpleasant sounding chord.

To solve this problem, the fourth or raised fourth is treated as an *ELEVENTH* or *RAISED ELEVENTH* and the ninth tone is voiced directly below. This harmonizes the melody with a third or minor third interval, thereby creating a pleasant sounding chord.

The following examples show the desirable ways of voicing the major and minor chords with a fourth step (eleventh) melody:

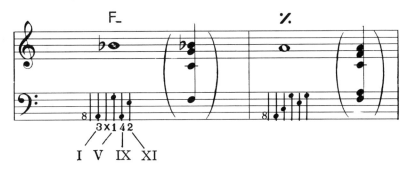

With the harmonization of the melody note, the chord now sounds pleasant and complete even though the third is still missing.

Example II

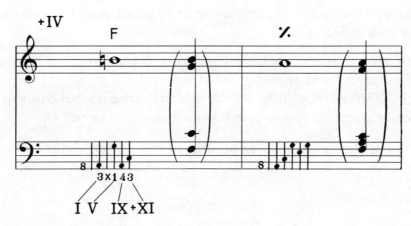

Example III
(minor)

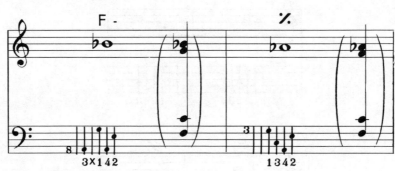

When the fourth step melody is indicated in a rhythm part it will usually appear as shown in the following examples:

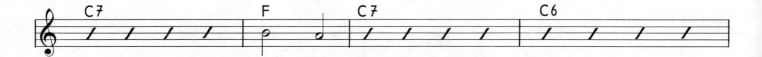

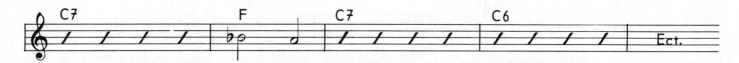

It is then up to the player to be able to correctly voice the chord accordingly. The forms shown in this study are, for the most part, all you will need. If a chord melody is being played, the root may be deleted:

The Eleventh and Minor Eleventh Chords

The eleventh and minor elevenths are extensions of the dominant ninth and minor ninth chords. Due to the lack of standardization of chord symbols, there has been a lot of confusion regarding the understanding of the eleventh and minor eleventh chords.

The following examples show a few of the ways that the elevenths and minor elevenths are written:

(a)   C aug 11

(b)   C 9 (aug 11)

(c)   C 9 (+11)

(d)   C 9 alt 11

(e)   C min 9 (11)

(d)   C -(9) (11)

By understanding the following simple format, the confusion over the eleventh and minor eleventh should be ended and the chord symbols standardized. The chart shows the numerical layout and chord symbol example of the eleventh and minor eleventh chord structures as accepted and used by most composers and arrangers.

(a)
$$\text{I} \quad \text{III} \quad \text{V} \quad \flat\text{VII} \quad \text{IX} \quad +\text{XI}$$
$$(\natural\text{III} = +\text{XI})$$

If the third is natural, the eleventh step will automatically be *raised*.

Chord symbol example: C^{11}

(b)
$$\text{I} \quad \flat\text{III} \quad \text{V} \quad \flat\text{VII} \quad \text{IX} \quad \natural\text{XI}$$
$$(\flat\text{III} = \natural\text{XI})$$

If the third is minor, the eleventh step will automatically be *natural*.

Chord symbol example: $C\text{-}^{11}$

Most authorities on the subject agree that these tonal arrangements should not be reversed such as using a minor third with a raised eleventh or a natural third with a natural eleventh:

(a) $\natural\text{III}$ = $+\text{XI}$

(b) $\flat\text{III}$ = $\natural\text{XI}$

There are, however, rare occasions when these rules will be violated.

In one situation (shown in the following example) the natural eleventh melody was used with a dominant ninth chord to produce a mode change from minor to major:

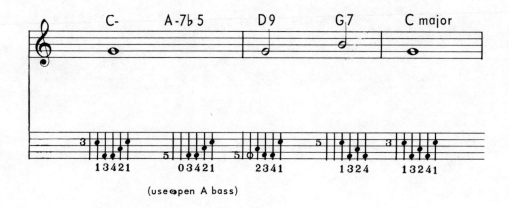

(use open A bass)

Such a situation is extremely rare and should not confuse the basic understanding of the eleventh and minor eleventh chord.

Basic Form Eleventh Chords
(Root Position)

I   III   V   ♭VII   IX   +XI

Chord symbol example: C 11

NOTE: Examples of phrases using the eleventh chord will be given after the minor eleventh section.

C 11

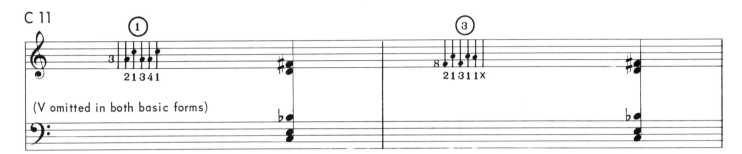

(V omitted in both basic forms)

F 11

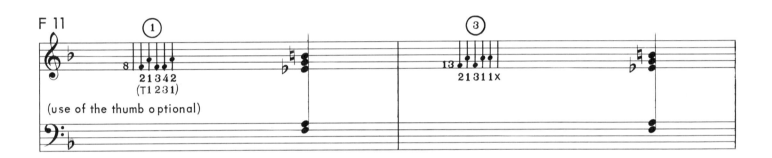

(use of the thumb optional)

B♭ 11

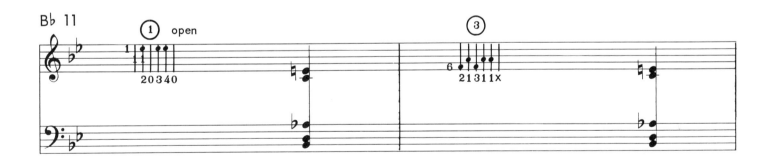

E♭ 11

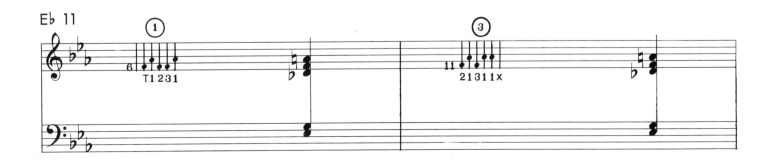

234

A 11

D 11

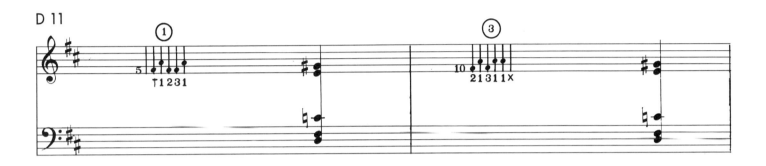

G 11

(Basic forms throughout entire cycle should be memorized)

Basic Form Minor Eleventh Chords
(Root Position)

I ♭III V ♭VII IX ♮XI

Chord symbol example: C -11

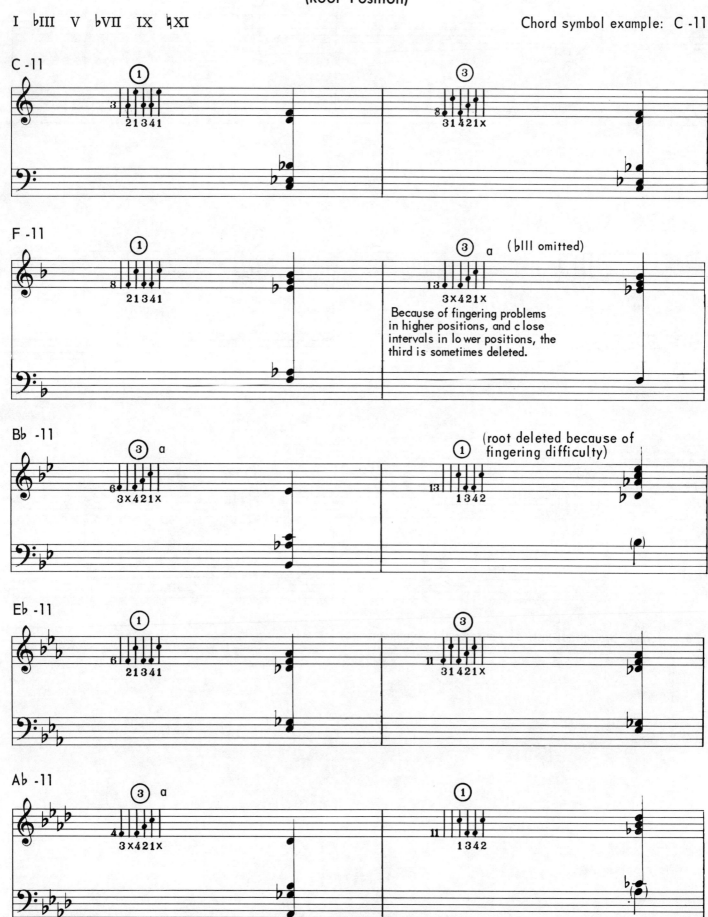

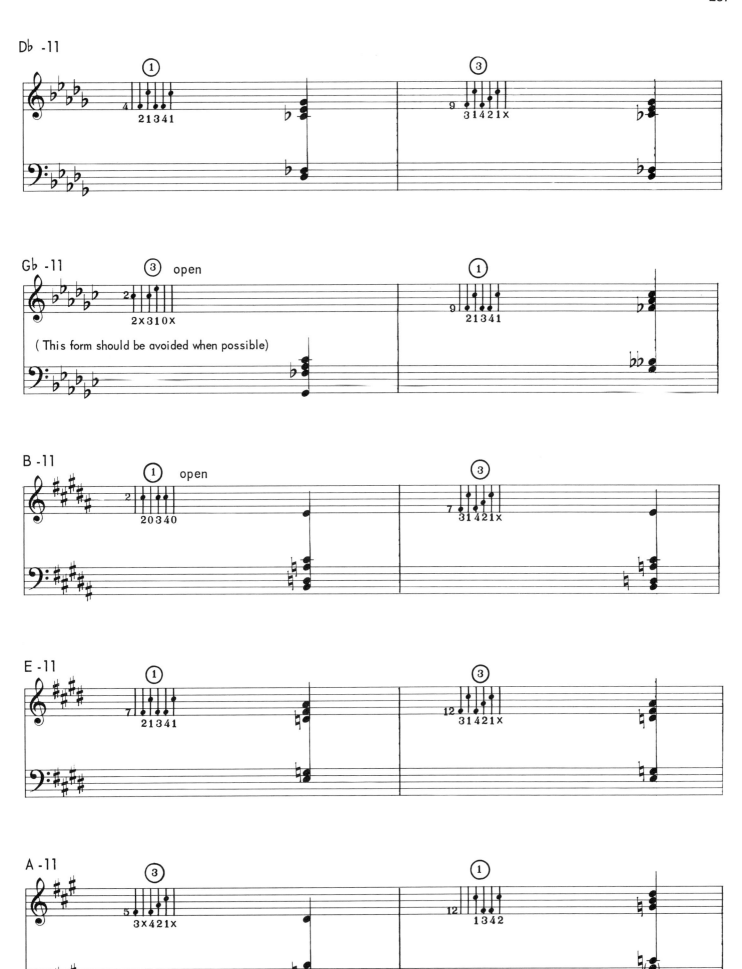

Db -11

Gb -11   ③ open   ①   2x310x

(This form should be avoided when possible)

B -11   ① open   ③

E -11

A -11

238

D -11

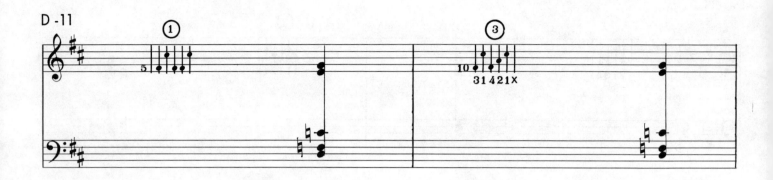

G -11

(Basic form throughout entire cycle should be memorized)

Frequently a complete eleventh or minor eleventh chord form can be played in the middle positions without having to use the incomplete chord forms in the lower or higher positions. This choice is especially important when playing rhythm or accompaniment.

Basic Resolutions of the Eleventh and Minor Eleventh Chords

The most common resolutions for the eleventh chord are to a dominant ninth, major ninth or six/nine chord *ONE HALF STEP LOWER.*

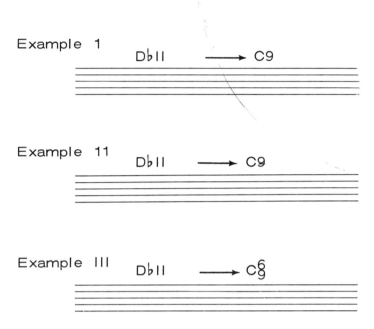

Being related to the polytonic 7♭5 chord, the eleventh is sometimes substituted for the dominant chord when the melody permits. The following is an example of such a substitution:

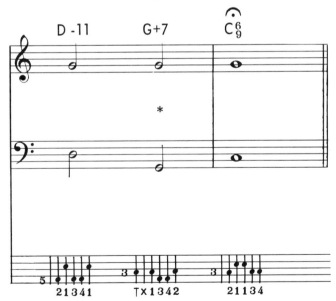

To avoid doubling the bass note with the melody note on the G+7, a D♭11 could be used as shown in the same phrase.

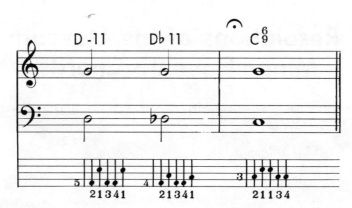

(You will note that the upper structure of the augmented seventh and the eleventh are the same.)

The most common resolutions for the minor eleventh
are to a IV 7 or to an eleventh one-half step lower.

Example I (IV step)

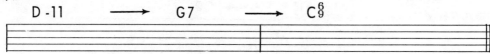

Example II (half step)

The following exercises use both the eleventh and the minor eleventh chords and are typical of the phrases using these chords.

Exercise I

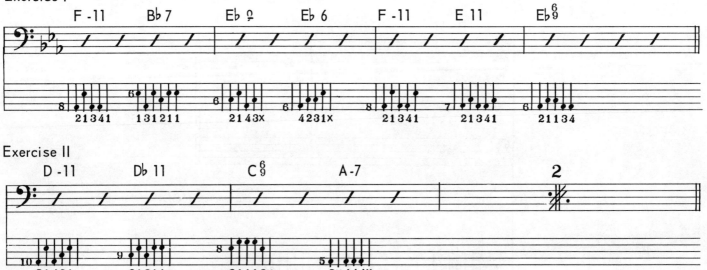

Exercise II

The following phrase uses the eleventh chord as an effective ending chord of a song.

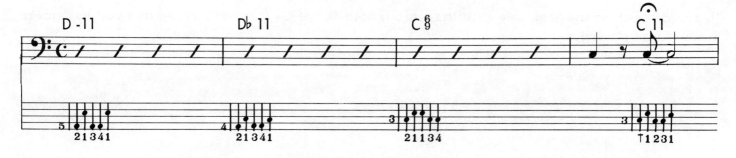

Alterations of the Eleventh Chord

ELEVEN FLAT NINE

Chord symbol example: C 11 (♭9)
C7♭9 (+11)

The following examples are common phrases using the 11♭9 chord.

Example I

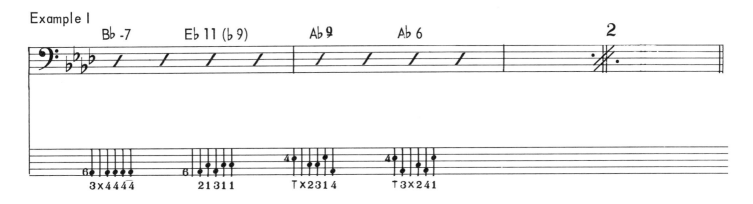

Example II

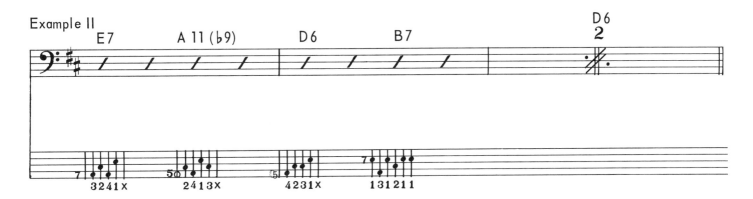

* Review diminished scale studies in conjunction with the eleven flat nine chords.

242

ELEVEN RAISED NINE

Chord symbol example: C 11 (+9)

C7 (+9 +11)

③ (root deleted)

21341

The following examples are common phrases using the 11 (+9) chord.

Example I

F -11   E 11 (+9)   Eb⁶₉   C9   F -11   E 11 (+9)   Eb⁶₉

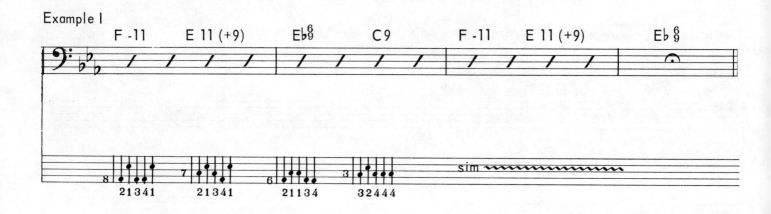

21341   21341   21134   32444   sim

Example II

B 9   Bb 11 (+9)   A⁶₉   F# 7   B 9   Bb 11 (+9)   A⁶₉

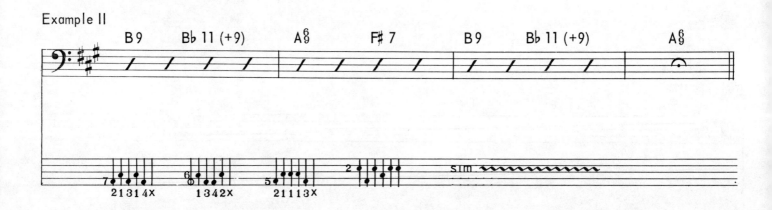

21314X   1342X   21113X   sim

Review diminished scale studies in conjunction with the eleven raised nine chords.

ELEVEN NATURAL SEVEN   Chord symbol example: C 11 (♮7)
                                              C 9̲ (+11)

This chord would, most likely, be used as an *effect* type chord and is frequently used as a closing chord of an arrangement, as shown in the following example:

Example I

Attention should be called once again to the simple components in the upper structures of these chords, like the minor triad in the upper structure of form ①. A chordal melody could be created to fit the last two bars of the exercise by inverting the "B – triad."

The Thirteenth Chords

The thirteenth chord is the extension of the eleventh chord, however, in its most common usage, the eleventh tone is omitted.

The thirteenth chord is structured: I III V bVII IX +XI XIII. It is the limit to which our tonal chord structures are extended.

The most common use would exclude the eleventh tone, but if the eleventh tone is used, it will be raised (+11). The ninth tone is sometimes omitted from the thirteenth chord also.

BASIC FORMS

(+XI omitted)

Chord symbol example: C 13

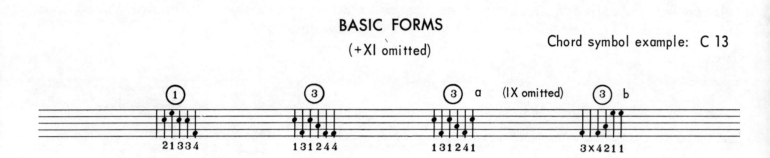

This form includes the +IX.

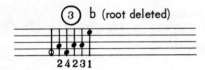

This being an extremely difficult fingering, just the upper structure of the chord can be used but would have to be located by the bVII on the bottom of the chord:

If a specific melody note is desired on top of the thirteenth chord, it will usually be notated:

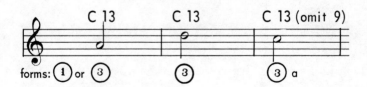

The basic forms studied here will omit the +XI and will include basic forms ① and ③ only.

D 13

G 13

(The basic forms throughout the entire cycle should be memorized)

Basic Resolution of the Thirteenth Chord

The basic resolution of the thirteenth (+XI omitted) is to a fourth step.

Example

The following examples show the thirteenth (+XI omitted) resolving in the most common way.

Example I

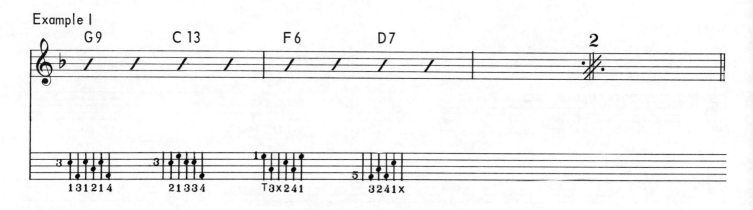

Example II

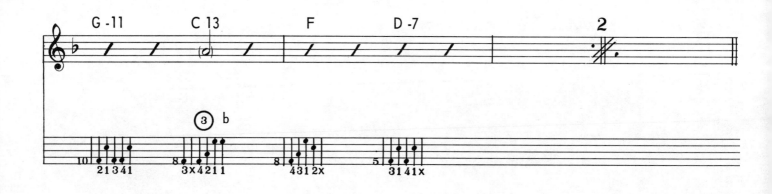

Example III

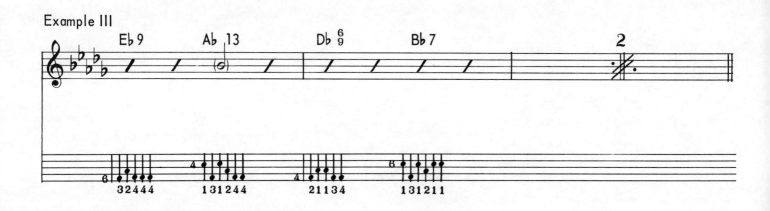

Resolution of the Thirteenth Chord with ⁺XI

If the +XI is included with the thirteenth chord it will usually resolve the same as the eleventh chord (to a seventh or ninth chord one-half step lower).

Example:

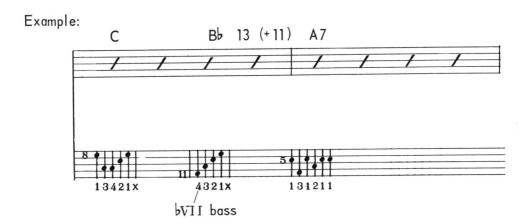

The suggested condensed forms for the 13 (+11) should be studied so that they can be readily located by association of the bVII on the bottom of the chord form.

Alterations of the Thirteenth Chord

THIRTEENTH SUS 4   Chord symbol example: C 13 (4)

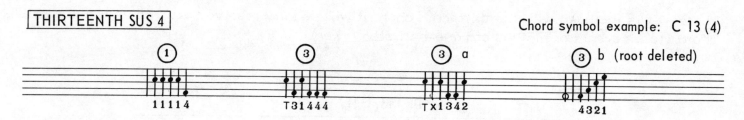

THIRTEENTH ♭9   Chord symbol example: C 13 (9)

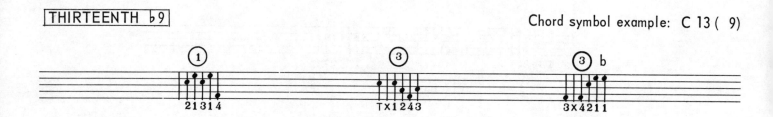

The following short phrases show the most common resolutions involving the thirteenth chord and some of its alterations:

Example I

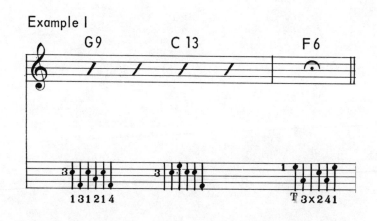

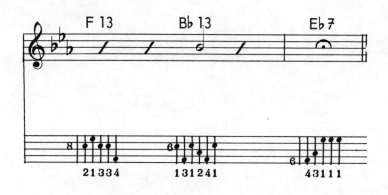

Example III

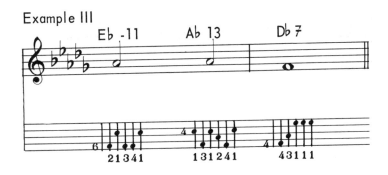

Example IV

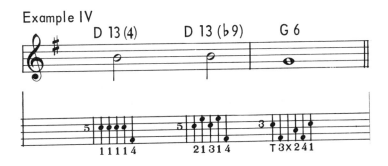

Example V

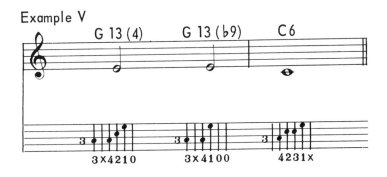

Example VI

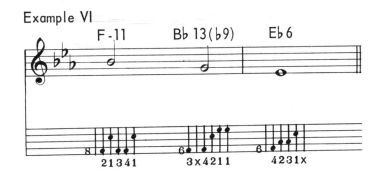

Example VII

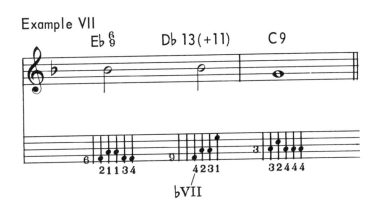

The Minor Thirteenth Chord

I ♭III V ♭VII IX ♮XI XIII　　　　　　　　　Chord symbol example: C -13

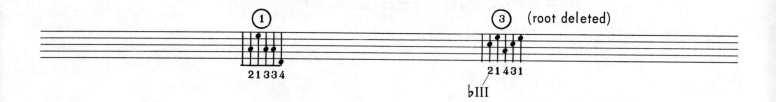

The minor thirteenth chord is not commonly used, and would only be used with a particular melodic situation such as the one shown in the following example:

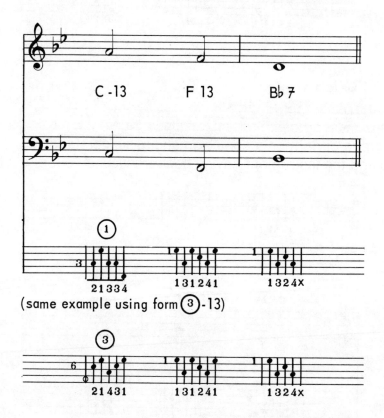

To simplify the fingering, the root could be deleted from form ① and fingered:

Of all the problems facing the serious student of the guitar, the harmonic knowledge expected of the guitarist is by far the most crucial. Students of the instrument have spent a lifetime trying to emerge from the quagmire of harmonic confusion and misunderstanding brought about by the use of chord symbols and the instrument having been transposed out of it's tonal perspective.

The topics covered in this book are as brief as possible without sacrificing thoroughness. The application of harmonies and theories covered in this book will have to be left to the individual, be it teacher or student. The important fact is, all of the material is useable, but more important is the fact that all accomplished guitarists and musicians are expected to know, thoroughly, all of the subjects covered herein.

This book has been written, solely, with the hopes that it may be of value to the serious musician as a supplemental text and reference to help put the harmonic and technical aspects of the guitar in some kind of order so that a clear understanding of these requisites may be made possible and practical.

JOHNNY SMITH

NOTES